Just 25 Days 'Til Christmas

An Advent Celebration for the Entire Family

REBECCA HAYFORD BAUER

Charisma
HOUSE
A STRANG COMPANY

Most STRANG COMMUNICATIONS/CHARISMA HOUSE/SILOAM products are available at special quantity discounts for bulk purchase for sales promotions, premiums, fund-raising, and educational needs. For details, write Strang Communications/Charisma House/Siloam, 600 Rinehart Road, Lake Mary, Florida 32746, or telephone (407) 333-0600.

JUST 25 DAYS 'TIL CHRISTMAS by Rebecca Hayford Bauer
Published by Charisma House
A Strang Company
600 Rinehart Road
Lake Mary, Florida 32746
www.charismahouse.com

Unless otherwise noted, Scripture in this book has been paraphrased by the author.

Scripture quotes marked NKJV are from the New King James Version of the Bible. Copyright © 1979, 1980, 1982 by Thomas Nelson, Inc., publishers, used by permission.

Scripture quotes marked TLB are from *The Living Bible,* copyright © 1971, used by permission of Tyndale House Publishers, Inc., Wheaton, IL 60189. All rights reserved.

Original artwork by Rebecca Hayford Bauer
Cover and interior design by Terry Clifton

Previously published as *The 25 Days of Christmas* by Victor Books, copyright © 1994, ISBN 1-56476-517-6.

"Holy Homes" by Jack W. Hayford. Copyright © 1983
Annamarie Music, admin. by Maranatha! Music.
All rights reserved. International copyright secured.
Used by permission.
Printed in China

Library of Congress Cataloging-in-Publication Data

Bauer, Rebecca Hayford.
  Just 25 days 'til Christmas / Rebecca Bauer.
       p. cm.
  ISBN 1-59185-567-5 (casebound)
  1. Advent--Prayer-books and devotions--English. 2. Christmas--Prayer-books and
devotions--English. 3. Family--Prayer-books and devotions--English. I.
Title: Just twenty-five days until Christmas. II. Title.
  BV45.B335 2004
  249--dc22
                              2004006058

04 05 06 07 08 — 987654321

To my husband,

Scott G. Bauer,

January 11, 1954–October 24, 2003,

with whom I was privileged to celebrate 29 Christmases.

I love you. I miss you.

I look forward to seeing you in heaven and celebrating the marvel of

Christ's coming for eternity.

Foreword

I'm smiling as I write—big-time smiling!

I'm about as joyous as Christmastime makes me, but it isn't even near that lovely season as I'm inscribing these words.

Still I'm "tickled," as we often say—but it would be more appropriate to say "tickled red-'n'-green" rather than "pink," because this is an introduction to a marvelously creative book about "Christmasing."

Please meet one happy handbook and also one wonderful woman. They are the reasons behind my smile and my being "tickled," because I have been asked to introduce them to you. Let's take the lady first.

Rebecca Bauer, whose creative genius and flair for turning the most imaginative idea into something practical anyone can do, is the author of this book. She is also my daughter, and that's probably the primary reason I am smiling, because I am one proud dad.

I am not only proud because she has done such a fine piece of work in this extremely useful, family enriching book, but I am also particularly thankful for the vision and the values that undergird her producing what I think you will find to be a timeless resource for making Christmas lovelier than ever at your house.

What you have in hand is the work of a woman whose motivation is to build a healthy, happy, and holy environment into all the life of her family. And she does this. As you read, you will find this wife-and-mother's vision applied to just one season, but believe me when I say, "She lives and serves these values all the time."

Woven into the fabric of these pages is more than merely bright, joyous ideas for celebrating Christmas in the true spirit of our dear Savior's coming. There are character-building concepts and life-deepening hints that will bring dimension as well as brightness to this precious season. Which is to begin my introduction of the book, too.

Here is one happy handbook designed to take the "weary" out of Christmastime's fuller-than-average schedule. I predict it's going to add new quantities of the genuine joy intended in the original Christmas to your heart, your home, and your family.

Just 25 Days 'Til Christmas is the overflow of the heart and hands of a young woman who grew up in a home where Christmas was celebrated with unabashed fun as well as undiluted meaning. As she and her husband established their own home, they carried this tradition to new and brighter levels of joy and happiness. And that makes me all the happier.

Christmastime was meant to bring us love—at every level; from creating the most boisterous, festive laughter and enjoyment to answering our hearts' most deeply whispered prayers. Here's a helpful guidebook, a format for a faith-filled as well as a fun-filled Christmastime observance. It's new evidence that every generation can find not only the happiness and excitement of Christmas, but can do so while keeping sensitive to its meaning and message.

—Jack W. Hayford
The Church On the Way
Van Nuys, CA

Introduction

Christmas is a joyous, bright, heartwarming, miraculous season. It is a time to dwell on the miracle of Christ's birth and delight in the warmth of family. However, Christmas is also a hustling, bustling time of year, and as a young mother, I found that my tendency was to hustle and bustle my children off…to their rooms, to Grandma's, outside—anywhere but where I was so that I could take care of the profusion of additional chores that accompany the season. There were other things to juggle at Christmas, too—school, soccer, carpool, even having to cook every night! Things that normally fit comfortably into our daily lives became major projects in December. But in my diligence to accomplish all of these responsibilities, I had completely missed the point! This was a time for us to work together, to play together, to celebrate and laugh together.

Christmas has long been called a season for children. But I had become so involved in the busyness that the children were set aside. I found myself so busy with doing things for them (buying gifts, planning surprises) that I wasn't spending time with them in giving, in baking, in decorating, in wrapping, and in teaching them about the miracle of Christmas.

My story has a happy ending! As I stepped away from the "urgent" and took a good look at the "important," I realized that what I really wanted was to give my children their first taste of what Jesus' coming really meant. I wanted to be the one who explained to them the story of salvation incorporated within the Christmas celebration. I wanted them to begin to understand the eons of time that had passed since God had promised Adam and Eve that the seed of the woman would come to bruise the serpent's head and He would redeem us back to Himself. I wanted them to get a grasp of the centuries under a law that no one could possibly fulfill; the darkness and futility of a life without God's continuous presence. And I wanted them to sense the joy of that first Christmas when into the world of sin, darkness, and futility burst the Son of God, the Light of the world, the Redeemer, God with us…Jesus.

Yet these things cannot merely be spoken. They have to be lived and breathed. One way to do that is to fill every Christmastime with so much joy and meaning that it becomes a natural part of a child's life, because it is a natural part of our family!

For many people, life in Jesus and joy are mutually exclusive. "Joy" is suspect because life in the love of God is reduced to rules and spiritless service. But "joy to the world" was God's idea. He said that spirituality and joy were supposed to go together! Scripture tells us that we are to "serve the Lord with joy and gladness of heart" (Deut. 28:47), that His joy will fill us with strength to accomplish what He has set before us (Neh. 8:10), and that "in His presence is fullness of joy" (Ps. 16:11).

This Christmas will be my first Christmas as a grandma! I look forward to celebrating with another generation and sharing the joy of Jesus' coming. My prayer for you is that the Lord fill your home with holiness and happiness this Christmas, and that this book help you to make a spiritual, practical, and emotional investment into the lives God has entrusted to your care.

—Rebecca Hayford Bauer

2004

For me, the blending of these two aspects of Christmas are best summed up in a song:

Holy Homes
Jack W. Hayford

Hang the lights, come and string the berries,
Make another ornament to trim the tree.
Have a bite of chocolate cherry,
Pour another cup of Mamma's Christmas tea.
Candles, holly, crèche, and angels,
Bells, and balls, and mistletoe.
Holy homes needn't be unmerry,
Jesus and His coming fill our hearts with glee.

Buy a goose, plan a feast that's dandy,
Bake a dozen pies and make the pudding plum.
Candied yams, buttered rolls, and chutney
Overflow the table with the best "yum-yums."
Sugar cookies, brandied fruitcakes,
Sticks of peppermint and gum.
Holy homes filled with bowls of candy,
Honoring the sweetest Babe that e're did come.

Come and kneel now, beside the tree now,
Let us open presents we have wrapped in love.
But while kneeling, a holy feeling,
Overflows our hearts with praise to God above.
His the gift that makes our Christmas,
Jesus, Savior of mankind.
Holy homes know He's made us free now,
Free to live in life, and free to live in love.

How to Use This Book

Dear Parent,

This book was written with the intention that it would grow with your family over a series of years, that it would be a servant to your family…not a hard taskmaster. In other words, don't feel obligated to do everything in the book every year!

Perhaps one year you will want to focus on the devotionals for the Sundays of Advent. Maybe another year you will want to follow the suggestions for preparing a nativity display or an Advent wreath. Choose several activities that will enhance your family life this year, and leave the others for another time.

Just 25 Days 'Til Christmas has three distinct features for you to tailor to your family's needs and personality each day. As you do, may this be a memorable Christmas filled with the joy of Jesus and the fun of the festivities!

FEATURE 1

Daily devotionals to equip parents to communicate their faith to their children and grandchildren through the story and symbols of the Christmas miracle, AND to provide children with the recognition that God has a plan for their lives that He will personally reveal to them.

FEATURE 2

An activity page containing hints to parents on how to incorporate their children into the Christmas planning and activities, and to offer ideas of things to do with their children to make Christmas fun.

FEATURE 3

A Christmas countdown filled with practical steps for holiday preparations, helping any family to move through the Christmas season with joy and anticipation—stress free!

When God first made people, the Bible says that He made them "in His image"! That doesn't mean that if we could see Adam and Eve we would know exactly what God looks like. But it does mean that He made us to be like Him; He made us holy.

A lot of people think that being holy means you have to be perfect and never make a mistake. But holy actually comes from the same word as whole. To be holy means that God made us complete.

When Adam and Eve disobeyed God, they were no longer complete because their hearts had become broken by sin. God, who is complete, could no longer have companionship with them because their sin had made them incomplete. But God had a plan! He planned to send His Son, Jesus, to earth so that He could take our sin upon Himself and we could once again be able to live in companionship with God.

This month, as you read through this book, we are going to be learning about God's great love gift to us—Jesus. First we will be talking about the events that happened around Jesus' birth. We want to have a clear picture of all the things that happened leading to Jesus' birth and how God brought about the miracle of our salvation.

Then, we are going to be talking about how our celebration shows us a picture of Jesus. Did you know that many of the things we do to celebrate Christmas teach us things about the Lord?

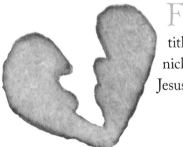

Finally, we will be learning about some of Jesus' names and titles. The Bible lists many different names for Jesus—kind of like nicknames. Learning about these names helps us understand why Jesus had to come and why we needed saving.

As you learn about the beliefs behind our celebration, remember that Christmas began in heaven! God loved us first!

Before we ever knew Him, before we ever heard of Him, actually, even before we were ever born—He loved us and had a plan to bring us into fellowship with Him. The Bible says, "Here is a matchless love, not that we chose to love God, but that He chose to love us and sent His Son to save us" (1 John 4:10).

December 1

Activity Page

Y{ou may want to begin this Christmas season by preparing an Advent calendar with your children. If so, this is the day to begin!

Advent calendars are an exciting way for children to actually see the countdown to Christmas. It builds anticipation, and as they get a little older and understand how a calendar works, it can even help cut down on the number of times you are asked, "How many more days until Christmas?"

There are lots of ways to have an Advent calendar. One fun idea might be to make or purchase an inexpensive manger scene and arrange a table-top display where you can add a new figure each day as you read through this book with your family. Begin by creating a stable out of a shoe box covered with wood-look paper. You could use the following figures on the days indicated:

Day	Figure	Day	Figure
1	Shoebox stable	2	Add hay to stable
3	Cow 1	4	Cow 2
5	Cow 3 or other animal	6	Innkeeper figure
7	Star	8	Angel
9	Shepherd 1	10	Sheep 1
11	Shepherd 2	12	Sheep 2
13	Shepherd 3	14	Sheep 3
15	Camel 1	16	Wise man 1
17	Camel 2	18	Wise man 2
19	Camel 3	20	Wise man 3
21	Donkey	22	Joseph figure
23	Mary figure	24	Manger
25	Baby Jesus figure		

In this way, you can make this Advent a time of joyful anticipation for your family.

Christmas Countdown

Are you going out of town sometime

during the holidays? Hotel and

airline reservations should have been

finalized by Thanksgiving weekend.

If you have not yet completed your

arrangements, finish them today.

The story of Jesus' birth has everything a really exciting story needs! It has a brave hero and heroine, long journeys, visits from heavenly beings, a bad guy, and a Prince who grows up to be the King.

The story begins thousands of years ago in a faraway village called Nazareth. One day the angel Gabriel visited a girl named Mary and told her that she would have a Son who would grow up to save everyone from their sin. Gabriel also went to Joseph, Mary's fiancé, and explained to him that this Child was a gift from God—the Son that Mary would have was actually the Son of God! Mary and Joseph both said yes to God's plan for their lives, and that makes them very, very brave.

Soon they had to make the long journey to Bethlehem to pay their taxes to the Roman government. These days we only have to mail our taxes from wherever we live. And if we have to go anywhere, we can just hop in our car and go. But Mary probably rode on a donkey, and Joseph probably walked. They went on a long, dusty road in a large crowd of noisy, jostling people who were also on the way to pay their taxes.

They finally arrived in Bethlehem, but the city was so crowded that there was no place for them to stay except in a barn, where Mary gave birth to her Son, Jesus. Even though He was born in a barn, angels sang. And even though His family was very poor, wise men followed a star to visit Him.

But then, wicked King Herod heard about the birth of this Child. He knew that the wise men had gone to visit Him and that they believed He would one day be King. Herod didn't like that. He didn't want anybody to be king except him, so he decided that he would find the Baby Jesus and kill Him.

That night an angel came and warned Joseph. He told Joseph to take Mary and the Baby and travel to another country called Egypt, where Herod would not be able to find them. Eventually Herod died, and Joseph took his family back to Nazareth, where Jesus grew up.

When Jesus was grown, He healed many people and preached to them about how much God loves them and wants them to love Him, too. But again, wicked people heard about Jesus. They saw the crowds of people who followed Him and believed in Him. They wanted all the people to follow them and do what they said, so they decided to kill Jesus—and this time they succeeded.

But this too was part of God's plan, because Jesus died on the cross for our sins. When He rose from the dead, He became the King of heaven. He promised that anyone who chooses to follow Him can receive great joy here on earth and life forever with Him in heaven.

December 2

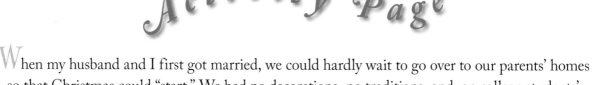

When my husband and I first got married, we could hardly wait to go over to our parents' homes so that Christmas could "start." We had no decorations, no traditions, and, on college students' salaries, no food!

But we soon realized that we were faced with the pleasant task of planning how Christmas would be at our house and starting our own traditions. So we borrowed a few from our parents, added some of our own, combined things from our two families, and came up with a "Bauer kind of Christmas"!

What's nice is that we can add to or change our family traditions any time. There are no rules! As our children grow and their interests change, we can add or subtract whatever we want so that Christmas is constantly new and exciting. But it still has the anchor of tradition woven throughout. Be prepared for the kids to offer their opinions, though! After my brothers and sister and I were all married, my dad asked if we ever had the traditional Christmas morning breakfast that we had grown up with. The answer was four very quick no's. To my parents' amazement, they found out that none of the four of us had ever liked it!

Starting a tradition can be as simple or elaborate as you want. One family I know has a tradition of always putting new toothbrushes in everyone's stockings. Another family tries to go to Disneyland each Christmastime to admire the Magic Kingdom decorations. One thing my husband and I have done is to save a Christmas stamp from each year since we've been married. The designs are always Christmas-themed, and it's a rather whimsical history of how things have changed since our marriage. We have them in a frame and add a new one each year.

Maybe your family would enjoy doing something like including a visit to a convalescent home or a visit to an elderly person in your church. Churches usually have extra events during Christmas. See if your whole family could help out in the child-care program one evening. Include your neighbors at Christmas. Take them cookies or coffee cake. Or, if you are really ambitious, have a neighborhood holiday open house.

Another good "tradition brainstorming source" is the library. Look up traditions from other countries. Browse though cookbooks and try some new Christmas goodies. Or borrow several craft books and make a few of your gifts this year.

And don't be afraid to borrow ideas from friends! If imitation is really the sincerest form of flattery, I'm sure they would be thrilled to share their ideas with you!

Christmas Countdown

If you are planning to do any mail-order shopping, all orders should be placed this week. Ask for an order number, and make sure you understand their return policy. Keep a record of your orders and the companies' telephone numbers in case there is a problem with anything. One friend gloated each year that all of his Christmas shopping was done by the end of November—all via catalog and from the comfort of his own armchair! It's definitely worth considering. Also, make sure that any airmail packages and cards to Europe and the Far East are sent out today.

God's Word is full of examples of God keeping His promises to people. The Bible calls them *prophecies,* and they are promises that God not only makes, but that He Himself also keeps.

God promised Abraham that he would have a son. Although it looked pretty unlikely to Abraham, he did have a son, and it was when he was one hundred years old! (And you thought your mom and dad were old!) Joseph was given promises by God. He saw that there was something great that God wanted to do with his life. Joseph's brothers laughed at him, but God kept His promise anyway. David knew he was to be king of Israel. The prophet Samuel had spoken a word from God! That wasn't very much comfort when David was hiding in the wilderness from King Saul, who wanted to kill him. But guess what: God kept His promise, and David did become king.

God also gave many promises about the coming of the Messiah—the Promised One who would bring salvation to all people. Hundreds of years before Jesus' birth, God told where He would be born: "Bethlehem, out of you shall come forth the One to be Ruler in Israel" (Mic. 5:2). God promised that Jesus' coming would free us from our sin: "All we like sheep have gone astray; we have turned, every one, to his own way; and the LORD has laid on Him the iniquity of us all" (Isa. 53:6, NKJV).

After Jesus was born, God kept giving promises. There were promises given to Joseph and Mary that Jesus would bring a light to the Gentiles (Luke 2:32). He made promises to the first Christians that they would minister in Jesus' name, and He would bless them (Mark 16:15–18). Paul's life was spared through God's promises (Acts 27:24–25). And the Bible even ends with the promise of Jesus' return (Rev. 22:20–21).

That's a lot of promises! But do you know what is just as exciting? The Lord wants to give you promises about your life! Sometimes they will be things to share with someone else to pray over, and sometimes they will be things to think about in your own heart. Either way, they will be things to give to the Lord and let Him fulfill…*because He always keeps His promises.*

Maybe God will put a big dream in your heart that people will laugh at, like with Joseph. Maybe it will be something that seems impossible, like with David. But 1 Kings 8:56 says, "Not a single word has ever failed of all God's good promises." And just as God kept His promises to all of those people, He will keep His promises to you, too.

December 3

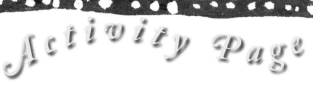

Activity Page

Advent means "coming," and an Advent wreath is a great way to keep our focus where it belongs—on Jesus' coming.

The Advent wreath originated in Europe and was a part of the religious celebration. Each of the four candles represents a different aspect of the events leading to Jesus' birth. Traditionally, they are the Prophecy Candle, representing hope; the Bethlehem Candle, representing faith; the Angel's Candle, representing peace; and the Shepherd's Candle, representing joy. The center candle is Christ's Candle and represents love.

The Advent wreath consists of a wreath or greenery-twined candelabra fitted with four candles. One candle is lit each Sunday leading to Christmas. Then on Christmas Day a fifth candle—usually larger than the other four—is placed in the center of the wreath, celebrating the birth of the Light of the world.

The celebration of the Advent wreath also includes reading scriptures showing both the Old Testament prophecies regarding the coming of the Messiah and the New Testament fulfillment of those promises.

Because Sundays fall on different dates each year, we've placed the devotionals that go with each candle throughout the book for you to use as your celebration determines. Listed below are the devotionals, along with a Scripture reading to go with each candle.

The Prophecy Candle	Devotional is on December 3. • Scripture reading: Isaiah 7:14; 9:6–7; Luke 1:30–35
The Bethlehem Candle	Devotional is on December 10. • Scripture reading: Micah 5:2; Luke 2:1–7
The Angel's Candle	Devotional is on December 17. • Scripture reading: Isaiah 52:7; Luke 2:8–14; 4:18–19
The Shepherd's Candle	Devotional is on December 22. • Scripture reading: Ezekiel 34:23; Luke 2:15–20; John 10:11
Christ's Candle	Devotional is on December 24. • Scripture reading: Isaiah 9:2; Luke 2:30–32

Christmas Countdown

Make a Christmas Master Calendar today. A little organization now will pay off all month long! Make sure you include everyone's activities. Are there any school or office gatherings? How about that soccer end-of-season party? Do you need to schedule any haircut or doctor's appointments? Does your daughter still have her piano lessons this month, or are they taking some time off? Get everything on your calendar. Other things to include: Are there any holiday meals or parties that will be at your house? Church activities? School Christmas program? Set aside decorating days now. Will you be having any out-of-town guests? Put their flight information on the arrival date on your calendar.

And while you are working on your calendar, make a few phone calls and arrange for a "babysitting swap" with a friend...and when you arrange it, be sure to put it on your calendar!

ary must have been a pretty amazing person! First of all, an angel comes and gives her a message from God. (I want to hear messages from God, but I think an angel would scare me to death!) Then, she agrees to do exactly what God has told her to do. (I'm willing to do that, but it's really hard sometimes.) Lastly, not only did she say she would obey, but also she *did* obey...and because she obeyed, God brought a blessing to the whole world! Just think—the Christmas story all began with Mary saying yes to God.

I think that makes her a pretty amazing person. But God wants all of us to be amazing people. Amazing people are people who obey the Lord. From Mary we can learn about three things she did that will make you the amazing person God wants you to be if you will do them, too! Mary had *listening ears*, *an obedient heart*, and *willing hands*. She lived in such a way that when God spoke to her, she could hear Him. She had a heart that wanted to obey, and her actions went along with what her heart wanted—she actually did what she said.

Now, God doesn't just let the years when we are kids go by, and then when we are grown up say, "OK—now that you are all grown up, you can figure out how you are going to listen and obey Me all by yourself." Instead, He gives us a whole growing up time to practice! We start learning to hear and obey God by hearing and obeying our parents. Learning to obey is a very important thing, and Mom and Dad teach obedience so that when you are older and God talks to you, you will already have learned how to obey, and you can obey Him. Right now, then, while you are young, you need to be learning to live with listening ears so that you can hear when Mom and Dad call you or give you instructions. Then you need to respond with an obedient heart and willing hands that are ready to obey your parents—and Jesus.

The best part, though, is that someday God will talk to you, and tell you what He wants you to do with your life, just as He did with Mary. Maybe it won't be through an angel, but He will talk to you. And when He does...obey Him. Because when we obey the Lord, He brings a blessing to us and to all those around us—just as He did with Mary!

Let's ask Him to help us right now.

Dear Jesus, give me ears to hear Mom and Dad. Help me to obey with my heart and my hands. And someday, when You speak to me about what You want me to do with my life, help me to hear and obey You, too. Amen.

December 4

Activity Page

There is nothing more Christmasy than baking cookies! It looks like Christmas, gets decorated like Christmas, smells like Christmas, and (best of all!) tastes like Christmas. So here are a few suggestions to help you get ready for the fun Christmas cookie-baking season!

Let your children help with choosing recipes. There will be a day later in the Advent season when you will actually bake the cookies with your children. (The information for that special day is included with Day 17 in this book.)

Cookie recipes like chocolate chip cookies and peanut butter cookies are quick and easy to make. (The store-bought tubes of cookie dough make this job even easier!) Or you could choose a recipe that's been handed down in your family or is traditional to your ethnic background. Make plum puddings, trifle, or scones if you come from a British background. Scandinavian countries make peppernut cookies, lace cookies, and aebleskiver. Magi cakes and torrone come from Italy. Mexico offers flan and sopapillas; France, mousse and tarts; and Germany, berlinkranzer and spritz wreath cookies. Go to the library, look up a little of the history of your family's background, and give your children a history lesson plus a cooking lesson!

Use the simple chart on the next page to plan ahead for your Christmas baking day.

Christmas Countdown

Get your plans together for baking today. After you have chosen your recipes, get them all in one place for easy locating. How many cookies (or other baking) are you going to have to do? Did you promise to bring something to one of the children's class parties? Are you planning to give any baking as gifts? Are you and your friends planning a "cookie swap"? Put all of that information with your recipes. Then start a grocery list with all of the ingredients that you will need.

Our Cookie Recipes	Our Cookie Shopping List	Our Scheduled Baking Day
1.		
2.		
3.		
4.		
5.		

Be sure to add baking days to your Christmas calendar. It will help to make the day filled with fun instead of frenzy.

Every day is a busy day when you are a kid! You might run around with the dog, help in the garden, read a great book, or do homework. Maybe you will skate, ride bikes, do chores, watch TV, and set the table. But no matter what you do, you are still listening. Even when there are all kinds of noise going on, if Mom or Dad calls, you will hear. You know why? Because you listen for the people you love. Even when there are a lot of other things going on, not only are your ears listening, but your heart is listening, too.

When Jesus would preach, He would sometimes end His sermons by saying, "He who has ears to hear, let him hear," and I think that's what He meant. He wanted people to be listening to the things He said—not just with their ears, but with their hearts, too. And that's true today—Jesus wants us to be listening for His voice.

He talks to people in many different ways. Sometimes He talks to us through His Word—the Bible. That's why you should be reading your Bible every day. When you read your Bible, the Lord can show you verses that tell you how to behave or how to solve problems. God also talks to us in our hearts and lets us know exactly what we are supposed to do in different situations. The Bible lists other ways that God talks to people. He talked to Joseph in dreams. The Bible says that He talked to Moses "face-to-face, as a man speaks to his friend." Samuel heard actual words, and David received beautiful songs from the Lord. Paul saw visions, and Elijah heard God's "still, small voice."

I don't know how the Lord will choose to talk to you, but He will always be with you and help you. You never need to feel lonely (even if you are the new kid), and you never need to feel afraid (even if it's thundering outside!). He will help you to make right choices about the things you do. He will remind you of the things you've studied when it's time to take a test. He will encourage you to do your very best at all times. And He will always tell you how much He loves you.

All it takes to hear His voice are ears to hear Him and a heart to love Him. God wants to talk to you—just as simply as Mom or Dad does.

Love Him. Listen for Him. He's waiting to talk to you.

December 5

Getting your annual batch of Christmas cards in the mail can be one of the most tedious jobs of the holidays. The repetition of signing, stamping, and sealing envelopes can all be a real test of patience. Yet there are ways to make it a family project.

First, get your Christmas cards together and devise a plan. Divide your cards up, and do a few each night. Or write your family letter tonight, copy it tomorrow, and then have a marathon card-stuffing evening. Try using an assembly line approach with each family member responsible for a different part of the job: Mom signs the cards, Susie puts them in the envelopes, Joey puts on a stamp, and Dad addresses them. I like to divide the job by task: write and copy the Christmas letter one day, sign all of the cards one day, stamp the envelopes one day, and so on.

In any event, the children can help by sealing envelopes, attaching return address stickers, and putting on stamps. Older children may even be able to address the envelopes. Involve the youngest children even if all they can do is hand you one envelope at a time for you to address. Don't tax their willingness to help, however. A toddler's interest in the job may only last for five envelopes. And make sure they wash their hands first. (Believe me, I have learned that one by experience!)

Another way the children can help is by putting together a Family Newspaper to put in each card. Have them write about their favorite event of the year, draw a pen-and-ink drawing to go along with it, and then sign their names. This gives long-distance relatives an opportunity to see some of each child's personality. If your children are younger, you could write the letter, while having them tell you what they want to say.

When my husband and I were first married, the cost of postage and cards was about a fourth of what it is now. But now, as then, I think it's a good relational investment. I could not possibly afford to send each of those people a gift, but when I compute the cost of mailing each individual card, it seems a small price to pay to let faraway friends and relatives know that they are always in my heart.

Christmas Countdown

Start your Christmas cards today! Hopefully you can get them all done in one day, but if you have a large family as I do, that probably isn't reality! My Christmas cards usually get stretched out over a week or two, but make the start today. To make big jobs happen, I usually subscribe to the "divide and conquer" philosophy. Here are the "divisions" to our family's Christmas card process:

1. Write, copy, and fold your Christmas letter.
2. Purchase stamps.
3. Update your address file. (Several years ago I invested the time to put my address list on computer. While the initial time output was considerable, I have saved time ever since! Each year I simply print out the labels, and I'm ready to go! Though I was raised with the idea that every envelope should be hand-addressed, our techno-society has begun creating new etiquette, which actually simplifies life. Enjoy!)
4. Stuff the cards and letters into the envelopes.
5. Have a "sealing-stamping-labeling" day.
6. Aim at having all of your Christmas cards in the mail by December 15.

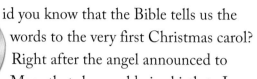

D id you know that the Bible tells us the words to the very first Christmas carol? Right after the angel announced to Mary that she would give birth to Jesus, she sang a song![1]

It shouldn't surprise us that Mary would sing her praise to God at such a time. The Book of Job says that God created the whole world while the angels sang praises. Psalms tells us over and over to sing praises to the Lord. It also tells us that praise makes us beautiful! Nehemiah says that praise makes us strong! And Isaiah says to sing to the Lord when He has done excellent things—which is all the time! So after the angel had come to Mary, she sang a song of praise and rejoicing. Her song also tells us the reasons why she was rejoicing:

First, she said that she was praising the Lord because, "Though I am not important, God has looked upon me." Mary knew that she could not do anything unless she had the Lord. She praised Him because even though she was helpless, God saw her and cared about her. Thank You, Lord, that You always take care of us! Mary recognized that without God's help she was nobody special. But look what she says next!

"From now on, everyone will say that I'm blessed!" Why? Because even though she knew she was no one special, God made her into someone special! And just as God had a plan for Mary's life, He has a great plan for each of our lives that no one else can do. That special plan will not only bless us, but will also bless people around us! Thank You, Lord, that You have a plan for my life and that You make me into someone really special.

Next, Mary praises the Lord because "He who is mighty has done great things for me!" She thanks Him because "He is merciful and compassionate"; He understands everything we face; "He has exalted" us and made us into someone special who can bless others; "He has fed" us; He always provides for all of our needs; "He is strong and helps" us; and "He speaks to" us.

When we hear Christmas carols this Christmas, let's remember the praise that was in Mary's heart when she sang that very first Christmas carol. There are a lot of good reasons to praise the Lord, but the best one is the same one that Mary had…Jesus.

Let's sing our thanks to Him right now!

1. Luke 1:46–55

December
6

Activity Page

Several years ago, my family fell into the habit of listening to secular radio. We weren't listening to "heavy metal"; we were listening to pretty love songs. But while I carry no brief against secular music, I did get a little tired of hearing my children going around the house singing, "I love you, baby."

One day I realized that if I surrounded my children with music that was spirit-strengthening, I would be living out the Lord's directive in Deuteronomy 6:6–7 (NKJV):

"And these words which I command you today shall be in your heart. You shall teach them diligently to your children, and shall talk of them when you sit in your house, when you walk by the way, when you lie down, and when you rise up."

Not only is music a great teacher, but it can also bring comfort, help us memorize Scripture, apply character traits, bring understanding of spiritual principles, minister freedom to our lives (Ps. 32:6–7), dispel the works of the adversary (2 Chron. 20:20–21), and allow God's creative majesty and full liberty to work in our homes and in our lives (Job 38:4–7).

Play music in the car and in the house! Learn some Christmas carols and go caroling. Sing a song together each night before bed. Sing a chorus of thanksgiving for your dinnertime prayer.

A couple of years ago following an earthquake, my children sang, "God is my refuge and strength…though the earth be moved" (Ps. 46:1–2). The Word in song banished fear and brought comfort to them. We have watched the power of spiritual songs break the grip of depression oppressing our home. We have seen God create new attitudes, new peace, new ideas, and even new study habits as we have given ourselves to praise in prayer and in song.

Our children will live out what we put into them. Let's put in things that establish eternal truths in their hearts.

Christmas Countdown

During this first week of the Christmas season, we are concentrating on getting the season organized and getting our families ready so that we can relax and enjoy the commemoration of the birth of Christ instead of getting caught up in the chaos of the commercialization of this glorious time.

GIFT LIST—List everyone; this is not the time to trust your memory! Also include any host gifts, office party gifts, and materials needed for homemade gifts. Are there gifts you have purchased throughout the year? Do you have ideas of what you want to buy for each person? Write those ideas on your list too, along with sizes needed.

PARTY PLANNING—List those parties your family will be hosting, as well as every party any family member will be attending. For the parties you will be hosting, plan your menus ahead of time, and make out your grocery list now so you can take advantage of sale prices throughout the month. Call people who will be attending your parties to make any food assignments now, and mark them on your calendar. On your grocery list, be sure to include ingredients for any food items that members of your family will be taking to the other parties they will be attending.

MISCELLANEOUS LIST—Make a list of all the miscellaneous things you need to purchase. Bring out your gift wrap supplies from previous years, and decide what more you need. Add wrapping paper, tissue paper, ribbon, and tape to your list. Don't forget packing boxes and postage for any gifts that must be mailed. Don't forget to put batteries and camera film on your list. And while you are at it, pick up some thank-you notes.

Which do you think is more important: Christmas or Easter? They are both important holidays. You get vacations from school for both of them. And they are both about Jesus. So how can you tell which is more important?

Well, Easter could never have happened if Jesus hadn't come at Christmas, because the reason He came at all was to save us. And without Jesus' sacrifice at Easter, His coming at Christmas would have had no meaning; it would just have been the birth of another baby. The two holidays are linked together! So the answer to "which holiday is more important" is BOTH!

Our Christmas tree tells the story of both! Of course, it reminds us that Jesus came as a baby, because it is the center of our decorations and gift-giving celebration. But it is also a picture of Jesus' cross. In fact, the Bible even calls the cross a tree! First Peter 2:24 says that Jesus "bore our sins in His own body on the tree" (NKJV). On the "tree," Jesus gave the ultimate sacrifice—His life—and when He did, His blood flowed down to the foot of the cross. In the same way, we lay our gifts to one another at the bottom of our Christmas trees to remind us of the greatest gift we ever received: our salvation.

The Christmas tree not only reminds us of Jesus' cross, but it also reminds of His promise to give us "everlasting life." We use evergreen trees at Christmas because they stay green all year long and don't show signs of withering or dying. In that way, our Christmas tree can remind us that Jesus said, "He who believes in Me has everlasting life" (John 6:47, NKJV).

The Christmas tree is also a picture to us of what God does in our lives when we accept Him! The psalmist wrote that the person who follows God's ways "shall be like a tree planted by the rivers of water…whose leaf also shall not wither; and whatever he does shall prosper" (Ps. 1:3). And Psalm 92:12 promises that "the righteous shall flourish like a tree."

This Christmas, when you look at your Christmas tree, don't spend all of your time thinking only about the presents you will be opening in a few days. Spend some of your time remembering what the tree is a picture of and thanking the Lord for the gifts that He has given us: the gift of Jesus' coming at Christmas and the gift of our salvation at Easter.

December 7

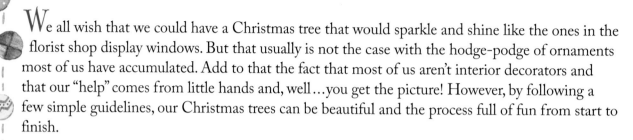

We all wish that we could have a Christmas tree that would sparkle and shine like the ones in the florist shop display windows. But that usually is not the case with the hodge-podge of ornaments most of us have accumulated. Add to that the fact that most of us aren't interior decorators and that our "help" comes from little hands and, well…you get the picture! However, by following a few simple guidelines, our Christmas trees can be beautiful and the process full of fun from start to finish.

Decorating the Christmas tree, of course, starts with getting the tree. Before you make your purchase, stand where you want to place your tree and get a firm idea of the size of tree you will need (both in height and width). When you figure height, don't forget to add the height of your tree stand and your tree topper. Then whether you chop a tree, buy a tree, use an artificial tree, or plant a living tree, make the setting up of it a fun first step in the decorating process.

Once you actually start decorating, follow these rules:

1. The lights go on first. (Hint: Clear lights show off colorful ornaments better.)
2. Next, put your tree topper on.
3. Now put on the garland. (Hint: Always work from the top to the bottom whenever you put anything on the tree.)
4. If you have bows to put on your tree, they go on now! I like bows because you can fill empty spaces with them. (Hint: If you don't use bows, try wrapping empty boxes to fill the empty spaces on your tree.)
5. The ornaments go on next. Put on all of one kind (or color) at one time for distribution purposes and to avoid color clumps. (Hint: Put the special or handmade ornaments on last. If you put them on first, they will be covered up with other decorations later.)
6. Remember to put smaller objects toward the top and larger objects toward the bottom. Also, put heavier objects closer to the center of the tree.
7. If you are using a real tree, don't forget to water your tree regularly. (Hint: Avoid spills by letting the children water the tree with ice cubes.)

Christmas Countdown

Everyone's calendar fills up so

quickly in December, so help

your guests plan ahead for your

event by sending out your party

invitations as early as possible.

When I was little, I liked to read stories about Jesus. He always seemed so kind and ready to help. I especially liked that He was brave enough to stand up to the "bad guys" because I knew I wasn't that brave. I also liked the fact that He loved everyone—especially children! I thought Jesus would be a great friend to have…and I wanted to be like Him. But I could only picture Him as a grown-up. If I was going to be like Him when I was a kid, I wanted to know what He was like when He was a kid!

We do know that He learned to be a carpenter from Joseph, so He must have had chores around the house and the workshop. I suppose He had to go to school. There is one verse, though, that describes Jesus as a child, and it gives us a pretty good idea of what He was like and how we can be like Him—even when we are still kids!

Luke 2:40 says, "And the Child [Jesus] grew and became strong in spirit, filled with wisdom; and the grace of God was upon Him" (NKJV). Later in that same chapter, we find out that Jesus had a solid grasp of Scripture even as a child. He was even teaching the teachers in the temple when He was twelve! It was Jesus' understanding of the Bible that brought that strength and wisdom and grace into His life—and it can do the same thing in yours!

Psalm 111:10 says, "The fear [or reverence] of the LORD is the beginning of wisdom; a good understanding have all those who do His commandments" (NKJV). Another verse says, "If you receive My words, and treasure My commands within you…then you will understand the fear of the LORD and find the knowledge of God" (Prov. 2:1–2, 5, NKJV). Psalm 119:28 asks the Lord to "strengthen us according to Your Word." Just think! The reason God gave us the Bible was to provide us with wisdom and strength!

Wisdom and strength are what go into our hearts when we learn the Bible, but grace is what comes out! Ecclesiastes 10:12 tells us that "the words of a wise man's mouth are gracious" (NKJV). In Colossians 4:6, Paul teaches us to "let your speech always be with grace" (NKJV). He also tells us to "let the word of Christ dwell in you…singing with grace in your hearts to the Lord" (Col. 3:16, NKJV).

So how can we become like Jesus? By being in the Word. We can read our Bibles. We can pay extra close attention when we go to Sunday school. We can carefully listen to the things that Mom and Dad teach us about the Lord. When we do that, the commandments that the Lord has given us in His Word will fill our hearts with wisdom and strength. Then the things we say and do will be full of the grace and kindness of the Lord, and every day we will become more and more like Him.

December 8

Activity Page

"Great peace have those who love Your law," promises Psalm 119:165. If there is anything that I could ask for my children throughout their lives it would be peace—spiritual peace, emotional peace, physical peace, international peace, educational, economic, vocational, and domestic peace. "Peace" is truly the great cry of our time, the longing of every heart, and the "impossible dream" of each generation. Yet this Scripture gives a clear-cut course of action for attaining peace in every arena of life.

Deuteronomy 6:7 further exhorts parents, "You shall teach them [God's commands] diligently to your children, and shall talk of them when you sit in your house, when you walk by the way, when you lie down, and when you rise up" (NKJV). What an assignment! And the beginning is the biggest challenge.

We begin to instill in our children a love for God's Word by loving it ourselves—and living it. I'm not talking about a letter-of-the-law legalism, but a living, breathing, life-changing, principle-shaping Word of God that is applicable to every situation we face.

Begin by involving the Word in your life. Are you in the Word daily? Do you apply its promises and commands to your personal life? We can tell our children that the Bible is an important part of life, but we also have to live it. Kids can spot a fake a mile away! Be in the Word every day. Draw on the spiritual nourishment that the Lord has provided. Let the Word of God in music fill your home and spirit with His peace and joy. As that happens in us, we can begin to impress a love for God's Word in the lives of our children.

When our children were small, we read a chapter in a Bible story book each day. We provided them with Bible music tapes as soon as they could talk well enough to sing along, and when they began to read, we gave them an easy-to-read Bible and encouraged them to read a portion of Scripture on their own each day. As teenagers, they accumulated preteen study Bibles, Bibles on tape, and even a comic strip Bible! We memorized Scripture together, played Bible trivia games at dinner, and applied specific verses to problems each of the children have faced. Being in God's Word should be simple, interesting, and fun!

What would your children enjoy? What will "hook" them into digging for the treasure that has been given to us in God's Word? There's still time to slip another gift under the Christmas tree! Ask the Lord how you are to introduce His Word to your children, and then watch as His peace begins to transform their lives into His image!

Christmas Countdown

Acting out the Christmas story can help the Bible come alive for our children. And it involves everyone—even family pets! This doesn't have to be involved, though. Bathrobes for costumes and a quick read-through of Scripture set the script. Then let the kids improvise!

Just don't let anyone try to ride the family dog!

One of my favorite things at Christmastime is to decorate the tree! But putting on the ornaments sometimes makes me think of fruit trees. You know—apple trees are covered with apples, orange trees are covered with oranges, and Christmas trees are covered with ornaments. I have wondered if maybe ornaments aren't "Christmas tree fruit"!

Each ornament is so beautiful, and many of them represent special things that have happened to us. Our family has ornaments from special vacations, ornaments from when each child was born, ornaments that were made at Sunday school. Maybe you have a lot of the same kinds of ornaments on your tree, too. They are special ornaments because each one represents a gift—the gift of a person or the gift of a special memory.

The Bible says that every good gift comes from God (James 1:17). Let's name some of the gifts that God has put in our lives. Can you think of any gifts that are represented by the ornaments that you have on your Christmas tree? Say those, too! And then, every time you look at your Christmas tree with its dozens of sparkling ornaments, thank the Lord that He has put so many good gifts into your life. God doesn't want us to stop there, though; He has an even bigger plan! He wants to decorate US!

There are other gifts that the Bible says God gives us. They're called the "fruit of the Spirit." The fruit of the Spirit are love, joy, peace, patience, kindness, goodness, faithfulness, gentleness, and self-control. Just as our Christmas trees are decorated with ornaments, God wants to decorate us with this wonderful fruit that makes us more like Him!

I think about God wanting to decorate me each time I decorate my Christmas tree. And I ask the Lord what new decorations He wants to put on me this year, because I want to have more every year! Would you like to have more decorations on you? Maybe you argue with your brother or sister, and God wants to decorate you with self-control and peace. Or maybe you always want everything to happen right now, and God wants to decorate you with patience.

What are you going to ask Jesus to decorate you with this year?

December 9

Decorating the house is the Christmastime chore that has always seemed the most time consuming to me, but I have found that varying our decorating plan from year to year has made a bigger-than-life-sized job much easier to handle. One year, we decorated a room each day until we were all done. We also usually decorate the Christmas tree on a separate evening from working on the rest of the house. Once following a very trying year, we decided to put up only our tree. Then there have been the years that we've entered the "annual decorating marathon" and stayed up until two in the morning getting it all done at once! But one thing has always held true: we try to include our children as much as possible.

On an earlier day in this book, we suggested that your family work together to decorate the Christmas tree. Now it's time to decorate the rest of your home. Make this a family affair. Children can hand Christmas garland to someone on the ladder. They can run errands and put up "unbreakable" decorations. Older kids can cut greens, carry boxes in and out, vacuum up pine needles, and help you set up the porcelain Christmas nativity scene! But when the kids are involved, there are a few rules to remember:

1. Keep the child's age and attention span in mind: big jobs for big kids, little jobs for little kids.

2. Let them work on a project that allows them to see a lot of progress. This isn't the time to ask them to sit and hold the glue gun for you! Let them wind the garland around the stair railing or help you set up the outside lawn decorations.

3. Make sure you give them complete instructions. Take time to explain everything. What may be obvious to you probably won't be obvious to them!

4. Allow them to have some decorations that are their own! Along with giving them ornaments each year that they hang on the Christmas tree, we let the children decorate their bedrooms. One year my kids made yards and yards of red and green paper chains, and we strung them around the bedrooms. Include an unbreakable nativity set for each child to put in his or her room so that they can reenact the Christmas story again and again! One year I went into my sons' room where they had set up a wooden nativity set. Was I ever surprised when I saw that along with the Holy Family they had displayed a whole herd of stuffed animals, some army men, and a plastic dinosaur!

5. Plan for breaks. What may be another project to us is just more Christmas fun to our children. Don't be a slave driver! Stop and admire everyone's work. Share some Christmas cookies. And relax, Mom! Enjoy what you've accomplished so far!

Christmas Countdown

When I decorate my home for Christmas, I like to start with the things that will give the biggest punch for the least effort. For that reason, I usually start with fabric items. (And one of the best things about starting with the fabric items is that they can easily be assigned to the children without fear of something getting broken.) Over the years, I have accumulated a lot of Christmas quilts and pillows. I throw them over all of the sofas and chairs, and have "immediate impact" in the house. Then we get the stockings hung up. That gives the mantle area its first Christmas touch. I also have a big bag of Christmas stuffed animals that get set around the house and in chairs. Finally, I keep remnants of Christmas fabric around. They can become tablecloths, backdrops for nativities, or tree skirts. Decorating doesn't usually happen in a day, but the house can get a quick start in just a few hours.

Have you ever wondered how God makes His promises happen? I used to imagine God doing something kind of mysterious that made everything go the way He wanted it to. But as I grew up, I found that the way God usually makes His promises happen is through great planning! Mary and Joseph are a good example of how that happens.

God had promised Mary that her child was to be the Messiah. Mary would have known enough of the promises about the Messiah's coming to know that He was supposed to be born in Bethlehem. That wasn't where Mary lived, and she could have spent all of her time worrying about how she could work it so that her baby could be born there. But she could not have made it happen on her own.

Instead, Caesar Augustus, the ruler of the Roman Empire, gave the reason for going there. God worked everything in such a way that Caesar suddenly decided that everyone should be taxed. In order to do that, they would have to go to the town of their birth. Joseph was born in Bethlehem, so to Bethlehem they went!

God planned the whole thing!

How to get to Bethlehem was Mary and Joseph's problem. But God used the things that were happening around them to get them where He wanted them to be when He wanted them to be there! And He did it so that He could cause a miracle to happen that would bring blessing to the whole world.

God wants to do the same kind of thing in each of our lives. We have talked before about God giving us promises. Sometimes when God gives people promises, they want to make the promise come true without His help. That never works. Whatever He promises, you will need His help for it to take place. You can't make it happen on your own.

That is what Bethlehem is a picture of: God bringing you to the place that He wants you to be so that He can do something great through you. God has different things for different people to do. And He tells people things at different times in their lives. No matter what God tells you or when He tells you, you can be sure that He will also bring about the perfect time for that to take place.

When God gives you promises, don't spend your time worrying about how they will happen. Listen to the Lord as He works in circumstances and talks to you through His Word. If you really want to do His will, He won't let you make a mistake. God will get you where you need to be when you need to be there so that He can work His great purpose in you.

December 10

Activity Page

I like to choose a theme and decorate our home a little differently each year. One year we used snowflakes; one year we made bows. One year we put little gold foil fans all over the place. While we might make one purchase to add to our decorations, it's challenging and fun to come up with a theme that will use the decorations we already have in a new (and inexpensive) way.

One way to add to your family's decorations is to make them. Bread dough ornaments are always fun to make. Or give the children baskets of fruit and nuts to put around the house. Have them make paper snowflakes to cover with glitter and hang from the ceiling or in the windows. Let them hollow out apples to use as candle holders. Christmas stickers and coloring books add to their supply of ideas and keep them busy decorating packages and coloring pictures. One year we even had an art gallery and let the children hang up all of the holiday art that they had made at church, school, and home.

In addition to the family decorations, our children had their own decorations. Every year we gave each of them a new Christmas tree ornament. These ornaments were often dated so that they could commemorate the year. But they also received ornaments as birthday gifts (for our December boy) and vacation mementos. The children often added small toys and projects that they made at church or school, too. We all enjoyed these ornaments in our home, and now that our children have their own homes and families, the ornaments went with them and are a part of their own home decorations. Best of all, these decorations already have years of happy memories attached to them.

Scent as a decoration is fun, too. Keep potpourri burning on the stove. Put a pot of water on, and add any combination of cinnamon, nutmeg, and cloves. Adding some sliced oranges or a little bay leaf is a nice variation. Also try putting some cinnamon sugar in a disposable pie pan and baking it in the oven for that "just baked" smell. Add a little ginger or nutmeg. Play with the spices and see what kind of combinations you come up with. One of my favorite smells is vanilla-flavored coffee, so I will occasionally bubble some of that on the stove just for the smell! I also try to buy several scents such as gingerbread, pine, or bayberry to spray all around the house.

Use your imagination and see what ideas you come up with to fill your home with decorations that delight every sense: see the tree, hear the music, smell the spices, feel the warmth, and taste the goodies!

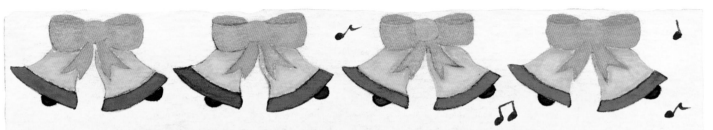

Christmas Countdown

Any packages you want to send by

parcel post within the continental

United States need to be sent today.

When Mary and Joseph first arrived in Bethlehem, there was no place for them to stay. Everyone sent them away except for one innkeeper who felt sorry for them and offered them his barn. It has always amazed me that Jesus—the Son of God and the One who would be the King of kings—was born in a stable filled with dirty, stinking animals, and that His first bed was a trough filled with hay.

It also seems sad to think that anyone would ever have turned Him away. Could the innkeeper have given Mary and Joseph his own room? Or could one of the villagers have seen that Mary was about to have her baby and helped her in some way? Instead, no one helped them, and they wound up in a barn.

Today, Jesus is still looking for a place to stay, but now He isn't looking for houses to live in; He is looking for hearts. That is why He came…to live in us.

Jesus said, "I have come that you may have life, and that you may have it abundantly." That means that He doesn't just give us "regular life"; He gives us extra special life! First, He comes in to live in our hearts. Then He fills us with so much of Himself that our lives become more than we could ever have thought! He fills us with more joy, more love, more hope, and more of Him! Everything that was in our lives before becomes better when we add Jesus!

He is looking for hearts to let Him in so that He can do new things in us every day. In a way, it's the same as what happened with Mary in that barn—she had something new happen with her, and the Lord wants something new to happen with each of us, too.

Your new thing probably won't be a baby. But, then again, maybe it will be! Maybe there's going to be a new baby in your family. Jesus will fill your heart with so much love that you will love everybody more—Mom and Dad AND the new baby!

Is there a new kid at school who is afraid or lonely? Maybe Jesus wants you to be a friend to that person. Maybe He wants you to pay more attention to your lessons at school so that you can become a better student—someone who is honoring the Lord in everything you do! Maybe you need to work on truthfulness or sharing or diligence. Whatever it is, Jesus will help that new thing happen in you!

December 11

Activity Page

In all of the decorating, don't forget the outside of your house! If you are fortunate enough to have snow for Christmas, you are halfway there! Your house already looks like a Christmas card! Build a family of snowmen on the front lawn. Or light your house in a way that will show off an icicle fringe or a snow-frosted fence.

Lights outside are a must at Christmas! And there are as many different kinds of lights and ways to put them on as there are people! There are different colors and sizes of Christmas lights. There are lights that go off and on in color patterns, or lights that twinkle like the stars. String Japanese lanterns across your yard, or outline your walkways with luminaries. My personal favorite look is large-sized colored lights on the house, and small-sized white lights on the shrubs. It's a look that I have never gotten tired of; I enjoy it so much that I finally asked my husband to put permanent hooks all along the roof line to make hanging the lights each year an easier process. (He grumbled at the time, but it has been easier ever since!)

Another common outdoor decorating idea is the use of greenery. Wreaths, pine cones, pine boughs, garlands, and gilded fruit are all beautiful outdoor decorations. One family I know even planted a large pine tree in their front yard and decorate it as their main Christmas tree each year; then they can enjoy its beauty both indoors and outdoors.

Other people focus on a specific style. Some purchase or build large-scale scenes to put on their rooftops or lawns. Still others add taped music to their outdoor decorations. You may want to do all of these or none of these, but whatever you decide to do, let your house look like Christmas!

Christmas Countdown

Christmastime presents us with a unique opportunity to reach out to neighbors that we may never have met. We live in an increasingly isolated society, yet during the holidays, people are more open to receive than ever before. Take advantage of that openness by preparing something special for your neighbors.

Here are some ideas:

* When you bake, make extra to share with your neighbors.
* Have the kids make some homemade Christmas cards to drop off.
* Plan a neighborhood open house.
* A small gift, such as a candle or small ornament, would be appreciated.

Mary and Joseph came into Bethlehem hot and dusty and tired from their long journey. Mary's baby was ready to be born, and they needed a place to stay. So they went to the most logical place—a motel or inn. But Bethlehem was so crowded with people coming into town to be taxed that the inns were all filled. Mary and Joseph were worried. They needed a place for their baby to be born!

And God provided one. It wasn't in a comfortable hotel or someone's house. It wasn't in a huge palace where you might think the Son of God should be born.

Everyone would like to go to a palace. It's beautiful and has gorgeous paintings and valuable furniture. But you can't just walk right into a palace. You have to be a very important person or a friend of the king to be able to go to a palace. You have to pass an inspection to make sure you aren't sneaking something in that will hurt the king. Then there are guards all over the palace who protect the king and who make sure that no one goes in an area that is off-limits.

Instead, Jesus was born in a stable—a place that isn't very comfortable or nice. A stable is dirty. You don't have to be anybody special to be able to go into a stable. Anyone can go there.

That is the lesson that God wants us to learn: He wants us to know that Jesus will go anywhere and that you don't have to be anyone super important or famous or rich to be able to come to Him. Jesus wants you. And He will do whatever He has to do to be able to have you come to Him—even be born in a dirty, stinky stable.

What is the hard situation that you are facing right now? Maybe school is hard for you, or maybe there is a bully at school who constantly teases you. Maybe your baseball team is the league champs this year…or the underdogs. Both of those extremes require strength of character to deal with in a sportsmanlike way. Maybe you just can't remember your times

tables. What if you really blew it on the final unit test? Or what if your project partner is a lazy student who doesn't help get very much of the work done? What will you do?

No matter what happens on any day, remember that Jesus is always there with you. When you don't know what to do, pray and ask Him to come right then and show you what to do. And He will…because Jesus will go anywhere that you are!

December 12

Activity Page

One morning I was thinking about my daughter and was overwhelmed with thankfulness for her. Later in the day, she walked into the room where I was. I turned to her and said, "Lindsey, this morning I was thinking about you, and it made me so happy that I just wanted to get you and hold you for a long time." She looked me right in the eye and said, "Well, why don't you?" So I did!

This incident brought back to mind something that a woman in our congregation once shared with our women's group. She was studying for a degree in marriage and family counseling and learning about the importance of touch. In her studies she had read that for a child to survive, he or she needs four loving touches per day; for that child to grow, he or she needs eight loving touches per day; and for the child to flourish, he or she needs twelve loving touches per day.

Our group of ladies decided that we would each make a conscious effort to give each of our children twelve loving touches each day. In my case, that involved thirty-six loving touches because I have three children. I was surprised throughout the following week how difficult it was to meet that goal! But as time went on, I got better at it, and my children began to respond to me with more loving touches of their own!

The abrupt words of my daughter made me realize that perhaps I was slipping in that area. It also made me realize how much children still need our touches, even as they grow big and become adults.

That day Lindsey and I went into the family room with a video of her choice, and I held her through an entire feature-length movie! I made additional efforts to caress the children's arms as I walked by, or to brush their hair back from their faces as they talked to me. Each morning when they woke up I tried to greet each of them with a long hug and a kiss on the cheek. I held their hands when we walked places together; I put my arm around their shoulders when we sat together. I didn't always keep count, so I don't know if I always reached the goal of twelve loving touches per child per day, but I think I did pretty well!

Maybe this month you'd like to hold your children for a while as you listen to their favorite Christmas CD or watch their favorite movie. Try holding their hands on a walk or give them extra hugs for no reason at all! What better time is there to express our love for one another than at this time of year when we celebrate God sending His love-gift to the world. And who knows…it might just become a habit!

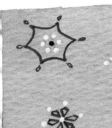

Christmas Countdown

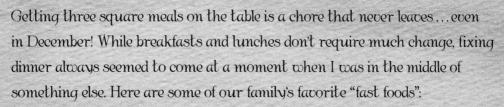

Getting three square meals on the table is a chore that never leaves…even in December! While breakfasts and lunches don't require much change, fixing dinner always seemed to come at a moment when I was in the middle of something else. Here are some of our family's favorite "fast foods":

- Roast chicken is always one of my favorites. Whether it's a whole chicken or pieces, you sprinkle it with garlic salt, add a few vegetables, pop it into the oven, and you have a healthy, easy meal with minimal effort.

- A favorite slow cooker recipe from a friend is to place a beef roast in the slow cooker and top with an envelope of dry Italian dressing and a jar of peppercinis. Cook the usual eight hours. It makes great sandwiches.

- Another slow cooker favorite is to simply pour your favorite barbecue sauce over boneless chicken pieces. This can be eaten plain or put on hamburger buns.

- Cranberry Chicken is also very easy. Combine a can of whole cranberry sauce, a bottle of Catalina dressing, and an envelope of dry onion soup mix. Pour over the chicken and bake.

Throughout the month, make double batches of casseroles and freeze meals ahead for super busy nights.

And when you're really swamped, call out for pizza!

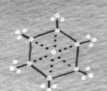

Do your mom and dad have a special name they call you? My dad used to call me "Punkin," and I have lots of special names for my kids—probably five or six for each of them! But did you know that Father God is the same way with His Son, Jesus? There are over three hundred names for Jesus listed in the Bible! It calls Him "Almighty" because there is nothing greater than Him. He is called the "Bread of Life" because He fills us, the "Door" because He is the way to God, the "Lamb of God" because He died for our sins, and the "Rock" because He is steady and unchanging. But one of the names that you hear a lot at Christmastime and in Christmas songs is Emmanuel, and it has a very special meaning. It means "God with us."

Before Jesus came, it was hard for people to know God. Of all the people in the world, only the Israelites knew about Him, and even they could only come to Him once a year. Only the priest was allowed to go into the holiest place one time each year to ask forgiveness for the whole nation.

But God made it possible for each person to come to Him by sending Jesus. John 1:14 says, "And the Word [Jesus] became flesh and dwelt among us" (NKJV). Jesus became a man so that we could see with our eyes what God was like. In John 14:9, Jesus said, "If you've seen Me, then you've seen the Father!" Jesus is someone we can touch and know. He is there with us. We can talk to Him whenever we want to! And because we know Jesus, we now know what God is like.

Isn't that an exciting thought? We can know God. He can be as close to us as our best friend. He knows us better than any one else! The Bible says that God cares so much about us that He knows how many hairs we have on our heads (Luke 12:7). He keeps each of our names before Him all the time (Isa. 49:16), and He is always with us (Heb. 13:5)!

That's what Christmas is all about. *Emmanuel: God is with us.*

December 13

Running errands" and "little children" seem to be mutually exclusive terms! But if you plan the day to include a few fun things for the kids and a lunch/rest time, things can go pretty smoothly.

If you are a stay-at-home mom, try to go early to avoid as many crowds as possible. If you work, the dinner hour is a less crowded time at the local mall! Then plan "chore" errands and "fun" errands. Take a list of exactly where you will be going and what you will be doing or purchasing at each stop, and put them in order ahead of time so that you don't have to retrace your steps. Also, take along some nonmessy snacks, such as raisins or nuts. If you don't want the hassle of having to stop for a meal, pack a fun "picnic" with Christmasy foods like peanut butter sandwiches on raisin bread, popcorn or trail mix, and candy canes for dessert. (And don't forget the diaper wipes for messy hands!)

Here are some errands to consider:

1. I go to the grocery store first because it's my favorite "one-stop shop." Besides shopping for all of my baking supplies, I can buy wrapping paper, ribbon, stocking stuffers, and even small gifts for someone's gift exchange! By stopping at the market first, I can sometimes eliminate several other stops.

2. Buy all of your Christmas wrapping paper and ribbon. Let the kids help you pick these. You'll be surprised at what good taste they have!

3. Do all of the Christmas shopping for Dad. Just wrap the gifts as soon as you get home to protect them from prying eyes, and make sure the kids understand exactly what "keeping a secret" means!

4. If your family follows this tradition, pay a visit to Santa Claus.

5. Stop at the toy store. The kids will like it, and you can get some good shopping ideas for them. Let them help choose gifts for any children on your list.

6. Do any "miscellaneous shopping." Find several small gifts to have available for office parties. Don't forget the boss. Purchase stocking stuffers.

Christmas Countdown

Now we are in the thick of things! Keep a running list of errands you need to run, and get them out of the way by using "time bytes." You could run a couple of errands during your lunch hour. Take advantage of the time during your son's basketball practice or your daughter's gymnastics class. Another great time for errand running is right after dropping the children off at school—the stores are still relatively empty at that time, and you are "out and about" anyway.

When I was a little girl, I heard someone say that our spirits were hungry for God. I wasn't sure what that meant, but I decided that it must be kind of the same as our bodies being hungry for food. When I got older, I found out that was exactly what it was like!

There is a place inside each of us that can't be filled up with food. You may think that when you eat it fills up all the places inside of you. But food can't fill up your spirit. We can't fill it up with soup and cereal and sandwiches; we have to fill it up with God. God made us to need Him, and if we don't include Him in our lives, then our spirits become hungry for Him.

When God created the first people, they were filled with God. But when they sinned, their spirits became empty and hungry for God. Ever since then, people have been trying to fill the hunger and emptiness in their spirits. And because God loves us, He made it possible for everyone to be filled with Him again.

God sent His Son, Jesus, to fill the empty place inside of us so that our spirits could be filled with God again. But to have that happen, we have to ask Jesus to come into our lives. Remember that Jesus said that He is the Bread of Life (John 6:48). He was saying that He knows our hearts are hungry and that He can fill them up, just as bread fills our stomachs.

Jesus, the Bread of Life, was born in a place called Bethlehem. Bethlehem actually means "the house of bread," or a bakery. What do we get from a bakery? (Bread.) What did God give us from Bethlehem—His bakery—that would fill our hungry hearts? (Jesus.) Just as we fill our bodies with food, we fill our spirits with Jesus, the Bread of Life.

Have you asked Jesus to come into your life? If you haven't, ask Him today. He wants to come live with you and fill your spirit with His bread—Jesus—so that your heart will never be hungry again.

December 14

Many things that are incorporated into our celebration at Christmas are both symbolic and prophetic. They remind us of the Old Testament promises regarding the coming of the Messiah. They symbolize Jesus' actual coming, reminding us that Jesus "made Himself of no reputation, taking the form of a servant, and coming in the likeness of men" (Phil. 2:7). What a miracle! What a cause for rejoicing and celebration!

But Jesus' birth can never be separated from His death and resurrection. Neither would have significance without the other, and Jesus provided us with the ultimate visual aid to help our children grasp the relationship between the two when He instituted the Lord's Table. While it does give us an opportunity to explain the sacrifice of Jesus' body, it goes way beyond that! At this time of year, the bread can be used to portray how Jesus took on human flesh to live with all mankind (John 1:14). And the wine, as a symbol of the Holy Spirit, becomes representative of the fact that not only did He come to "dwell among us" but also to dwell within us (Rev. 3:20).

Use this opportunity to teach your children the guidelines found in 1 Corinthians 11:17–26. Observance of the Lord's Table isn't a time merely to mourn again over the fact that Jesus had to die, although a certain sobriety and reverence are always appropriate. But "Do this in remembrance of Me" is a call to rejoice in all that Jesus has done for us in providing salvation and forgiveness and healing. And, yes, all of that was provided for us because of His death on the cross. But Jesus doesn't call us to live in grief any more than a beloved relative who died would want for us to dwell only on the fact that they are gone. The Lord's Table gives us an opportunity to celebrate the triumph of the cross, not just mourn over the fact of the cross.

As you serve the Lord's Table to your family, don't feel disqualified. Scripture says that we have been made a nation of kings and priests unto our God (1 Pet. 2:9; Rev. 5:10). However, if you do feel hesitant to serve Communion yourself, plan to participate in Communion together as a family some time at church this month. In either case, allow a spirit of joy and reverence to fill your home and hearts as you rejoice together in God's greatest gift to each of us.

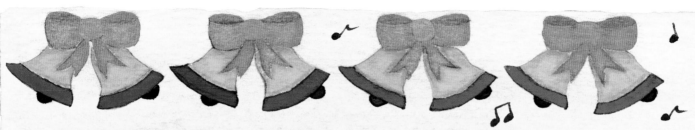

Christmas Countdown

If you are a working parent, holiday chores and errands can present their own set of unique challenges. A little planning ahead will help smooth the way for a joyous Christmas celebration.

If you need time off of work for your child's Christmas play or a field trip, let your boss know as soon as possible.

Are there other holiday arrangements that need to be made with carpool or after school childcare? Schedules can be a little more erratic during December. Make sure to stay on top of the changes.

Lunchtime can be the perfect shopping time—either online or at the local mall. Make those minutes count to get things accomplished! This would also be a great time to work on Christmas cards.

Lunches for your child can be fun in December as well. Tuck in a Christmas print napkin or holiday cookies when you make lunch.

Simplify other chores:

- There's nothing wrong with pre-made cookie dough for your holiday baking!
- Send e-cards, instead of traditional Christmas cards, to friends and family whose e-mail addresses you have.
- Decorating your home doesn't have to be a burden either. Not everything has to go up every year. Decide what you have time for and just do that.

And you can set the mood with scent and sound. Play lots of Christmas music, and keep scented candles burning.

Christmas is called a time of peace. People talk about it. You have probably seen doves or other kinds of peace symbols on Christmas cards. But what most people don't talk about is why this is a season of peace.

When the angels announced Jesus' birth, they sang, "Peace on earth!" because one of the names for the promised Savior was the "Prince of Peace" (Isa. 9:6). They were proclaiming that Peace had now come to rule on earth! Many people thought that meant that as soon the Messiah came, He would "protect all the good guys and get rid of all the bad guys" (or maybe "throw them in jail") like some kind of cartoon super hero! But Jesus came to bring a different kind of peace. He gives us a peace that stays with us no matter what. God's kind of peace fills your heart and makes you feel loved. It is a peace that only God can give, and there is nothing else that can take its place.

Many people try to fill that place with something else. Do you know kids who are angry and who bully other kids? They are trying to fill that place with power. Some kids try to fill that place with friends or food or lots of toys and clothes. They are trying to fill that place with acceptance. Other kids try something good like to fill that God-shaped place with getting good grades or being helpful. But even if you try filling that place in your heart with good things, it will be like using the wrong key in a lock. It can never open the door to God's peace, and it will never make you completely happy, because you have tried to fill it with something that doesn't fit right.

Have you ever tried to open a door with the wrong key? It might look like the right key. It might even go into the lock. But when you try to turn it and open the door, nothing happens. That is what it's like when we try to fill our hearts with something other than God: we become frustrated, unhappy, and upset. But when we fill our hearts with the Lord, we find peace.

Jesus said, "In Me you may have peace. In the world you will have hard things happen to you; but be of good cheer, I have conquered the world" (John 16:33).

That means that no matter what difficult situation we face, we can have peace. If you aren't facing something hard right now, thank the Lord. But if you are, ask the Lord to help you. Talk to your mom or dad, and remember, no matter what you face, the Prince of Peace is right there with you.

December 15

The gift of god is eternal life. Romans 6:23 The

Activity Page

December is a great birthday month! When our oldest son was born in December, it gave me a whole new outlook on Christmas: a new understanding of the practical things Mary went through (can you imagine riding on a donkey when you are nine months pregnant?), of the travail that had to take place so that God's gift could be given to us, and of the awe of seeing a new life brought into the world.

But on the other hand, the busyness of the season can mean that a December birthday can inadvertently be set aside or lost in the holiday hustle and bustle. I have heard "December birthday" people complain about no party, no celebrations, and sometimes even no gifts because their birthday gifts would be combined with their Christmas gifts.

If you have a family member whose birthday is this month, plan to make it an extra-special day. On our kids' birthdays we always tell the story of the day they were born. They hear about funny things that were said, how long it took, the exact minute they were born, and how happy we were to have them. And we always remind them, "I'm glad that you were born, and I'm glad that Jesus gave you to me."

But because this is a December birthday, we do a few things that are different. We try to coordinate some of our traditions as a family with Brian's birthday. First, because our evening schedule in December is usually so packed, we will celebrate his birthday and open gifts at breakfast. We will either have a special breakfast at home or go early (before school) to a restaurant with a breakfast smorgasbord. We will also usually buy and decorate our Christmas tree that day.

But there are tons of other ideas for December birthdays! Maybe go caroling and sing happy birthday at every house. Or plan something totally zany for a party—one year our son Kyle wanted to color eggs at his birthday party—it didn't matter that the birthday wasn't anywhere near Easter! Maybe a special Christmas tree or snowman-shaped birthday cake is what your child would like to accompany his or her favorite dinner. Or you could all wear Santa hats at the birthday party! Whatever you choose to do, make the day special so that your birthday boy or girl knows that you are glad that he or she was born!

Even if there isn't someone in your family having a birthday this month, we all know Someone whose birthday IS this month! Maybe a birthday party for Jesus would be a good reminder for us all of the joy that was in Father God's heart at Jesus' birth. I'm glad that He was born...aren't you?

9:15 Every good gift and every perfect gift comes

Thanks be to god for His indescribable gift! 2 Corinthians

Christmas Countdown

Mom—take a little time for yourself today. In the middle of a very hectic season, not only do you deserve it, but also you owe it to your family. I've always believed that the investment I make in my own well-being benefits my whole family because you can't give what you haven't put in. On days that I feel as if I'm running on empty, I realize the truth of that concept. My patience is low. My words can be sharp. Everyone in the family wants to "keep their distance."

So today, take some time for yourself. Maybe a long, hot bath would be nice. Spend fifteen minutes reading something fun. Or maybe Dad would even take all of the kids to McDonald's tonight and give you a longer break. In any event, keep yourself in peak condition for the holiday marathon by "putting something in" today.

There are lots of bells around at Christmas! We sing "Jingle Bells" or "Silver Bells." At church we might hear, "I Heard the Bells on Christmas Day." People hang bells on their doors and Christmas trees. And there are whole strings of bells on street decorations and window displays.

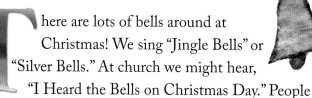

In our country, bells are important because the Liberty Bell is a well-known symbol of freedom. Did you know that it even has a Bible verse on it? It has Leviticus 25:10, which says, "Proclaim liberty throughout all the land to all its inhabitants." Whenever that bell was rung, it was supposed to remind people that they were free.

While the Bible doesn't say much about bells, it does teach us that true freedom comes only through Jesus. That is why He came—so that He could make us free. The Bible says that wherever the Lord is, there is freedom (2 Cor. 3:17). That means that if we've asked Jesus into our hearts and He lives in us, we can be free!

Just as the Israelites were slaves in Egypt, the devil wants to make us slaves by convincing us that wrong things are OK to do. You might decide to tell a lie. Or you might cheat on a test at school. Or you might steal a candy bar from the market. But it is always a trick. What the devil wants to do is trap you into a habit that you can't stop...so that you become a slave to lying or cheating or stealing.

Here's how it happens: Ask Mom to wrap one string of thread around you. You can break that pretty easily, can't you? If she wraps five or six strings of thread around you, you could probably break it, but it would be a little harder. But if she wrapped nineteen or twenty threads around you, you probably could not break it at all.

Every time you give in to doing something wrong, Satan wraps a string around you.

It may not seem like very much at first, but if you continue doing it, and he continues wrapping strings around you, it will become a habit you can't break. If there is something in your life that you can't stop, then you have become a slave to that. You aren't free anymore.

The good news is that if Jesus has made you free, you are really free (John 8:36). There's no question about it! Because Jesus came (which is what we are celebrating now), died for us, and rose again, He has the power to break all the strings that are around us!

So whenever you hear a bell—a sleigh bell, a church bell, a Salvation Army bell, even a doorbell!—remember that Jesus came to make us free, not just in our country, but in our hearts.

December 16

Activity Page

Christmas vacation has started! And while you may have more to do than the hours of the day allow, time hangs heavy on your kids' hands! Help the children to use this time constructively! When our kids were home at Christmas time, we encouraged them to read, draw, and play outdoors. But we also had them work on projects that benefited the whole family.

One day during a Christmas vacation, my kids were surprised to find out that I planned for them to sand and prime the garage door so that Daddy could paint it after work! You may not want to take on that ambitious of a project, but there is always yard work to be done, and even mundane jobs like raking leaves can take on a new look when you do them together...and promise hot apple cider for a job well done!

Let the children help you with the housework. By the age of ten, each of my children could clean the bathrooms, vacuum, and mop floors (almost) as well as I could. Not only has it helped them learn the importance of working together as a family (as well as mastering some very important college survival skills!), but also it was a huge help to me in weeks that were unbelievably busy. I also found that they could straighten and organize their own closets and dresser drawers pretty well on a particularly "boring" day!

Make a batch of salt-flour dough and let the kids make ornaments, small figurines, or even a nativity! Between the making, drying, and painting, they'll have a nice-sized project on their hands. Or plan a project that uses fabric. Let the kids color a tree skirt made from a sheet. Give them fabric paints, and let them use their imagination. Or have them decorate T-shirts for different members of the family. Any of these would be great gifts as well as being a fun project.

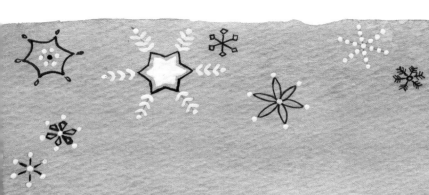

Christmas Countdown

Even though this is the age of overnight

airmail (a handy, albeit expensive,

convenience), you may want to allow

extra time for shipping's busiest month

of the year. Try to get any last-minute

packages in the mail no later than today.

When I think of Christmas, I think of angels! They are mentioned in Christmas carols. We put them on the tops of our Christmas trees. They are on Christmas cards. And they are in the nativity sets that we put on the mantel over the fireplace or on tables specially decorated in honor of Jesus' birthday.

Angels do play a big part in the story of Jesus' birth. Throughout the Christmas story, angels bring messages to quite a few people. In fact, the word *angel* means "messenger." An angel came to Mary to announce that she would be the mother of the Messiah. An angel told Joseph not to worry, that Mary's Baby really was going to be the Savior. An angel warned the wise men not to go back to Herod. And we know that a whole choir of angels announced Jesus' birth to the shepherds.

But the angel's announcement to the shepherds didn't start out with a whole choir.

Throughout the Bible, every time God sent an angel with a message, only one angel came. But at Jesus' birth, a whole choir came! Some have even wondered if maybe all the angels of heaven were so excited about Jesus' birth and God's plan to save everyone, that they could not contain themselves. They just burst out into praise!

God wants us to be praisers and messengers, like the angels, too.

The Bible says that the Lord lives in the praises of His people (Ps. 22:3). When we praise the Lord, we are actually building a place so that the Lord can live with us! When we praise the Lord, it also helps us to "proclaim the praises of Him who called" us from darkness into light (1 Pet. 2:9). Praise helps make us free (2 Chron. 20; Acts 16:25). Psalm 147:1 says, "It is good to sing praises to our God" (NKJV). And Jesus even said that through little children comes perfect praise (Matt. 21:16). He wants us to be praisers!

We are also to be messengers. Mark 16:15 says that Jesus commanded His followers to go to the whole world and give everyone God's message. If we are Jesus' followers, then He also wants us to give people His message. Sometimes we can be His messengers by telling people how to know the Lord. Other times we are His messengers by being kind and showing Jesus' love. Sometimes we are His messengers by praying for someone who is sad or sick or scared.

Let's decide today that, like the angels, we will be God's praisers, and God's messengers, too.

December 17

Activity Page

Have you had Christmas Baking Day yet? Involve the children by letting them get out ingredients, measure, put away ingredients, stir, lick spoons, cut out cookies, lick fingers, grease cookie sheets, put cookies on cookie sheets, lick bowls, wash bowls, and decorate.

The only drawback to having the children help out is that their enthusiasm sometimes makes the mess bigger! So be prepared with an extra dose of patience and a sink full of soapy water so that fingers, bowls, and counters can be cleaned up quickly. My kids helped by putting ingredients away as soon as they were measured out. This kept the counters clear and spills at a minimum. I also had my children wear old, oversized T-shirts in place of aprons to keep their clothes clean.

Get your recipes out and ready to use. Because there is the risk of drips and rips, you may want to cover them with clear adhesive self-stick paper first. Maybe you can hang them from a bulletin board in your kitchen, or tape them to a cabinet door so they can be seen easily, but not in the direct line of fire for those drips.

Along with those recipes, let your children try some "artistic" cookies. Make sugar cookies, and let the kids cut them into shapes. (Encourage them to keep trying even if the cookie dough stretches and Rudolph comes out looking like a giraffe!) Then along with frosting and sprinkles, let them try painting their cookies. (Paint cookies before baking.) You can make cookie paint by combining an egg yolk and food coloring. Add a few drops of water as necessary for a good painting consistency. Then let them go for it!

Plates of cookies are always fun gifts to give and to receive. Make up a few to give to office staff, neighbors, and school teachers. You'll find that not only did you spread Christmas cheer when you made the cookies, but also you spread more Christmas cheer when you gave them away!

Christmas Countdown

Let the kids decorate the car for Christmas

(of course, with some "don't obstruct

the driver's view" rules). If you run as

many errands as I do, you will enjoy

the Christmas cheer "on the road"!

Have you ever noticed that when you open a closet door, the room you are in doesn't get darker? Instead, the closet gets lighter! That's what the verse in John means when it says, "The light shines in the darkness; the darkness can never put it out!" (John 1:5). "The Light" that verse was talking about is Jesus! Jesus came to fill our hearts with light. And He promises that if you will open the door of your heart to Him, He will come in and make it light! He will do for us exactly what happened with the closet.

Before Jesus came, the world was in total darkness. That doesn't mean there was no sunshine, but that people's hearts were dark with sin, and there was no light to show them how to find God.

Before Jesus came, there were no pastors or missionaries. There were priests and prophets, but they taught that someday the Messiah—the Savior—would come and help them find God again. Then into this darkness, Jesus was born.

The Bible calls Jesus the *Light of the world*. He is the Messiah that the prophets said would come someday. He is the One who would give us a light to find our way back to God. If you are lost and can't find your way, what do you use to find your way around? A light! That's why God sent Jesus and called Him *a light*...so that Jesus could help us find God and not be "lost in the darkness of sin" any more.

When we put lights on our house and Christmas tree, or put candles around the house at Christmastime, it's to remind us that Jesus came to be our light. The next time you are driving around and you see a Christmas tree or some beautiful lights on a house, you will know why they are there!

Because Jesus is the Light of the world!

December 18

Activity Page

This evening, give the children a visual picture of what you read about today. Turn out all the lights in your house and see how dark it is. Then light just one candle. It's amazing how much light one candle throws! Then turn on the Christmas tree lights and any other candles you may have around the house. The room will turn into a shimmering, glowing dwelling place of light. It's beautiful!

Or go out and look at Christmas lights! My favorite way to do this is with all the car windows down. I guess it's my "city version" of a sleigh! Bundle everybody up, provide bags of popcorn, and enjoy looking at lights, eating popcorn, and singing every Christmas carol you can think of! And, if it's cold enough, you may want to consider a cup of hot chocolate before bed.

The Jewish celebration of Hanukkah is another way to celebrate the coming of the Light. Hanukkah is also called the *Festival of Lights*, and much of the celebration centers around the lighting of the menorah each of the eight nights. The candles stand for courage, justice, and hope, and the commemoration itself stems from a period in history when the Jews not only faced extermination, but also were being forced to worship pagan gods. Through the leadership of the priests, God worked mightily in their behalf, and they miraculously triumphed! (Check the library for more information on this meaningful observance.)

Let the kids share again what they've learned about Jesus being the light of the world, and have a family candle-lighting ceremony, symbolizing not only the coming of Jesus but the overflow of His life into your family and home. It's a simple, yet powerful picture of what Jesus came to do!

Christmas Countdown

In the reality of life, not every Christmas is merry. Death, sickness, and divorce impact all of us at some dimension. Family disagreement can infect a celebration. And yet, the Lord always extends hope…life…peace.

In the middle of whatever you or a loved one may be facing this year, let me encourage you with a lesson that the Lord taught me as my family faced our first Christmas without my husband. The Lord pointedly told me to "choose life." That first Christmas was only weeks after Scott's death, and I would literally wander the house aimlessly. As Christmas neared, the Lord challenged me, that in the face of death, to do the things that chose life.

So I put up lights! I bought Christmas gifts! My children and I planned new traditions! We celebrated the Life-Giver! After all—that is what Jesus' coming was intended to do. Through Him, death is swallowed up by life!

This Christmas let me encourage you to choose life!

If you're facing a death-dealing situation, fill your home with worship!

Turn on the lights! Choose the life that Jesus offers. At all times and in every situation, He is there to bring redemption and hope.

If your kids aren't with you this Christmas, plan something special to send with them. Send a card for each day that they open like an Advent calendar. Or plan a special celebration when they get home. Instead of focusing on time apart, focus on the joy of having them in your life.

If you're facing an illness, either in your own life or in the life of a loved one, cling to Jesus. He is the Rock! He is our strength! I don't say these words tritely, but out of the experience of finding how true they are. He is the only place to build.

Some people put a big, bright bow on top of their Christmas tree. Other people put a beautiful angel. We put a star on our tree. We chose to put that instead of one of the other things because we wanted to remind ourselves that everything about the Christmas celebration is supposed to point to Jesus. That is what the star did at the first Christmas…it pointed the wise men to Jesus!

The Bible also says that "Star" is another name for Jesus! Moses prophesied in Numbers 24:17 that "a Star shall come out of Jacob" (NKJV). And in Revelation 22:16, Jesus Himself said, "I am the Bright Morning Star."

Sometimes people put stars in too important of a place. Just as in the Christmas story where there was an actual star that guided people to Jesus and a Person who was called a star, there is the same thing today. There are people we call "stars" on TV or in movies, but they don't shine like Jesus. Some people rely on the stars in the sky to show them how to manage their lives. But the stars can't tell you what to do with your life! Not the ones on TV or the ones in the sky.

Scripture says that while nature is beautiful, its purpose is to point us to the Lord (Rom. 1:20). The psalmist talked to God, saying, "When I consider Your heavens, the work of Your fingers, the moon and the stars, which You have ordained, what is man that You are mindful of him, and the son of man that You visit him?" (Ps. 8:3–4). In other words, he asks, "When I see Your majesty displayed in creation, O Lord, why would You bother with me?" Yet God has poured out His love on us, and the stars are to help point us to the Creator.

Other people turn to people who are called "stars"—movie stars or rock stars. Sometimes they make these people so important in their lives that they become more important than God. Yet Scripture reminds us many times that no one can compare to the Lord! No one else, no matter how captivating or attention-getting, can complete us as the Lord can.

Then as we follow Jesus, who is the Bright and Morning Star, He lights our path! Second Peter 1:19 tells us that as we walk in Jesus' light, it causes "the morning star [to rise] in our hearts," so that as we continue to walk in God's light, our hearts grow bigger to love Him more every day. I want that in my life. Don't you?

December 19

Living in Southern California, my children did not have a lot of experience with freezing winters or snow. If we got one morning of frost it was a novelty, and we all ran outside to look at the white roofs! But even as young children they discovered that in our culture, "Christmas" and "snow" go together. We see it on Christmas cards, TV specials, and decorations. In fact, every kid seems to love snow!

So plan some time this month to take a break and have a special snow outing, whether that time is a short hour and a half after work one night or an all-day weekend event. You may live in a climate like ours where you can go to the snow for an afternoon. One year, our "snow day" took a total of four hours. We drove to some nearby mountains and went sledding, ate an icicle, built a snowman, and threw a few snowballs. By then the kids were cold enough to go home!

If you live in an already-cold climate where snow doesn't carry the novelty that it does in Los Angeles, try something totally different: clear off that picnic table and eat a (quick) dinner of chili, cornbread, and hot cocoa or apple cider! The neighbors may think you are crazy, but I guarantee you that your children won't forget it! Top your evening off by watching a Christmas video together in front of a roaring fire.

Even if you live in a desert climate, you can do something related to snow. Some places "import" or make snow that can be enjoyed during the Christmas season. I have even seen some families spray paint tumbleweeds white and build a desert-style snowman! Or maybe make your own snow in the form of homemade ice cream!

Maybe the extent of your snow day will be to add to your Christmas decorations. You could set up a snow scene decoration on the dining room table. Maybe cut out cotton to put on your window sills to create a snow effect. Or use this day to put "snow" on your Christmas tree.

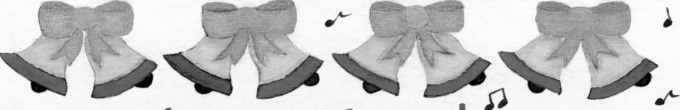

Christmas Countdown

Stocking Stuffer Ideas

Of course, there is always the good ol' standbys of candy and fruit. But I always liked to put lots of little presents in the stockings, too. Here are some suggestions:

INFANTS
- Rattles
- Teething biscuits
- Jars of baby food fruit
- Bibs

PRESCHOOLERS
- Socks (our kids loved this!)
- Small stuffed animals
- Balls of any kind!
- Mittens

ELEMENTARY-AGE CHILDREN
- Toothbrush (a stocking tradition at our house—everyone gets one!)
- Legos
- Calendar
- Art supplies

TEENS
- Makeup
- Everyone should get a little toy!
- CD
- Key rings (especially if they just turned 16!)

ADULTS
- Flavored coffees
- Golf balls
- Earrings or a watch
- Wallet

My husband always got pickled herring in his stocking … but I don't expect most people to think that's a treat! However, everyone has some special treat they would love to see turn up in their stocking!

This month you have read about the connection between the gift of Jesus' coming at Christmas, and the gift of our salvation at Easter. But another connection between the two of them can be seen in the colors of Christmas.

The colors most often used are red, green, gold, and white. We use those colors in our decorations and in the clothes we wear. Those colors burst out in stores and street decorations and Christmas cards. It seems that in December, the whole world has turned red and green! And there is a natural explanation as to why we use those colors.

The red and green come from the plants that are living at this time of year: evergreen trees, holly with its bright red berries, and poinsettias. White, of course, is from the snow that covers much of our country in the winter. And gold not only is one of the gifts that the wise men brought to Baby Jesus, but it is also a color that belongs to a king—which Jesus is. Besides, gold is just a fun color to celebrate with because it's bright, shiny, and happy!

The Bible talks about colors too, and in them we again see the story of our salvation.

Isaiah 1:18 promises that "though your sins be as scarlet, they shall be white as snow." It's a perfect picture of what Jesus did for us: He has forgiven us of our sins, and He has washed us so that we are now clean and pure before God. (See Psalm 51:7.) God also promises to clothe His people in white garments. Revelation 7:14 says that the saints "washed their robes and made them white in the blood of the Lamb" (NKJV).

Then, because we have been made clean through Jesus' blood, God makes us like a green tree that lives forever before Him. Jeremiah 17:7–8 says, "Blessed is the one who trusts in the Lord, and whose hope is the Lord. For he shall be like a tree planted by the waters, which spreads out its roots by the river…[its] leaf will be green…nor will [it] cease from yielding fruit." (See also Jeremiah 11:16.)

Finally, the Lord promises us a crown of gold because, through Jesus, we too have become God's children! David sang about our salvation in Psalm 21:3 and said, "For You meet him [that's us!] with the blessings of goodness; you set a crown of pure gold upon his head" (NKJV). The Bible also uses gold to describe heaven (Rev. 21:18); our beliefs (1 Pet. 1:7); and the Word of God (Ps. 19:10).

This Christmas as our celebrating fills you with joy, let the colors of our celebration also fill you with joy as they remind us of God's great gift to us through Jesus.

December 20

Santa Claus is a uniquely American character. While his origins may stem from St. Nicholas (who is known as the patron saint of children) and the Dutch Sinter Klaas, Americans took him and made him completely their own. In the frontier days of the prairie and the Far West, Santa Claus was even portrayed riding a pack mule!

But among believers, Santa Claus has become the subject of much controversy. And with good reason! Once the Bible and "religion" were thrown out of the school, there was no one else to focus on at Christmas. Santa Claus became the center of the season. People no longer greeted each other with "Merry Christmas," but with "Happy Holidays." "Getting" not "giving" was basic to the season as materialism took over. Of course, the merchants picked up on that, and now Christmas decorations are out almost before school starts in September!

What is sad, however, is the fact that children have a natural inclination toward wanting to pretend—and, yes, even believe in these fantasy characters. From Mickey Mouse and Tony the Tiger to the pot of gold at the end of the rainbow, children want to believe in the magical. Personally, while I don't remember ever believing in Santa Claus, I honestly believed in wishing on a star! Fantasy is a part of childhood! And it is unfortunate that our society has forced us into a position of having to choose between the foundation of our faith and the enchantment of imagination.

But the question still remains: what do we do with Santa Claus? Many Christian parents fear that if their children grow up believing in Jesus and Santa Claus, when they find out Santa Claus isn't real they will question the reality of Jesus as well. That can be a genuine dilemma for some people.

With our children, we decided to keep the fun of Santa at Christmastime. While the focus of our celebration has never been on Santa, we do go visit him at the mall, and my kids are still sure that they heard sleigh bells in the sky one year!

But we have always told them the truth. From their earliest years we told them that Santa Claus was pretend. They didn't listen to us because they wanted to believe that he was real! But as they got older and learned that he really was imaginary, they discovered something else: Mom and Dad had always told them the truth. About Santa Claus *and* about Jesus!

All of us, as Christians, are diligent to not let society rob Christmas of the holiday's true meaning, but neither should we allow it to rob us of the season's childlike fantasy!

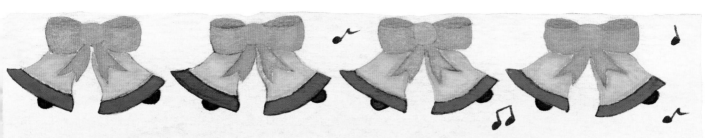

Christmas Countdown

Are you having out-of-town guests staying at your home during the holidays? Here is a checklist of things to think about as you prepare:

- Have you figured out sleeping arrangements?

- Is anyone staying with you who has special dietary needs?

- Do you need to purchase or borrow extra bed or bath linens?

- Are there any "visit only" rules that the kids need to know about? (Maybe about bathroom use; are they going to be sleeping somewhere other than their own beds; etc.)

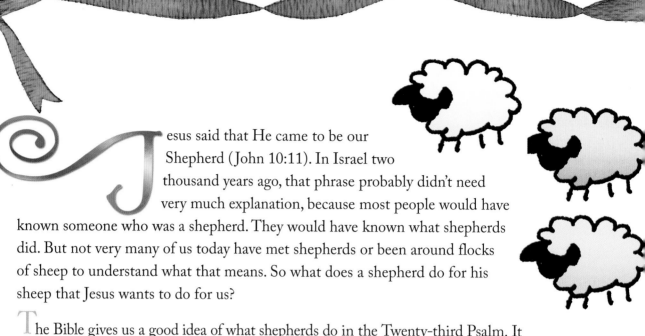

Jesus said that He came to be our Shepherd (John 10:11). In Israel two thousand years ago, that phrase probably didn't need very much explanation, because most people would have known someone who was a shepherd. They would have known what shepherds did. But not very many of us today have met shepherds or been around flocks of sheep to understand what that means. So what does a shepherd do for his sheep that Jesus wants to do for us?

The Bible gives us a good idea of what shepherds do in the Twenty-third Psalm. It was written by David, who was also a shepherd. And David writes that shepherds do eight things in Psalm 23 (NKJV):

1. "The LORD is my shepherd; I shall not want." [The Shepherd provides for all the needs of the sheep.]
2. "He makes me to lie down in green pastures; He leads me beside the still waters. He restores my soul." [He gives them safety and rest.]
3. "He leads me in the paths of righteousness for His name's sake." [He leads the sheep.]
4. "Yea, though I walk through the valley of the shadow of death, I will fear no evil; for You are with me; Your rod and Your staff…" [He protects the sheep.]
5. "…they comfort me." [The Shepherd comforts the sheep when they are afraid.]
6. "You prepare a table before me in the presence of my enemies." [He feeds the sheep, even in difficult situations.]
7. "You anoint my head with oil; my cup runs over." [The Shepherd pours oil on the sheep so their wounds can be healed.]
8. "Surely goodness and mercy shall follow me all the days of my life; and I will dwell in the house of the LORD forever." [The Shepherd promises that the sheep will always be with Him.]

So Jesus is saying that He wants to be our Shepherd; He is telling us that He wants to do those things for us! How? He promises to provide everything we need. He feeds us when we read our Bibles. He comforts us when we are afraid and gives us peace by making His presence real to us. He helps us know where we are supposed to go and what we are supposed to do with our lives. He protects us. He heals us when we are sick in our bodies or hurt in our hearts. And He promises that He will live with us and never leave us alone.

Isn't it great to have Someone to do all of those things for you? Moms and dads try, although they can't always be with us.

But Jesus promises to always be with us. It's why He came!

December 21

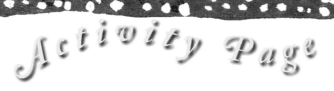

Activity Page

Have you ever made a gingerbread house with your kids? How about gingerbread men? In the middle of a hectic holiday month, it's nice to take an afternoon simply for doing something fun with the children. You need it, and they need it. And even in the midst of a much-needed break, another project can be accomplished. An afternoon spent on a gingerbread house or gingerbread men can yield a dining-room centerpiece or gifts for the neighbors. I realize that this sounds like a somewhat daunting project, but it doesn't have to be hard!

If you are home all day and have tons of baking talent, you might want to tackle a genuine gingerbread house! I tend to go an easier route on a project like this. Maybe some of these "quicker" versions will be better for you and provide just as much fun.

At Christmastime many markets and department stores carry gingerbread house kits that have everything prepared for you down to the last candy that goes on top of the chimney. All you have to do is put it together. Or you could make simple houses out of graham crackers and frosting. Try sticking the graham crackers to milk cartons for instant "houses," and build a whole village! My daughter didn't want to even make houses…she just wanted to decorate graham crackers. In a "technical" gingerbread house, everything must be edible. But if frosting is difficult for you to work with, use paste…just remember not to eat it!

Try building a log cabin out of candy cane sticks. Buy premade gingerbread men, and let the kids stick on chocolate chip eyes and buttons. You could even make something as simple as marshmallow snowmen complete with toothpick arms and candy corn noses!

Christmas Countdown

Only four shopping days left! But

to make your holiday as relaxed

as possible, try to have all of your

shopping out of the way today.

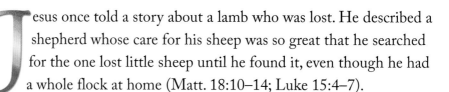

Jesus once told a story about a lamb who was lost. He described a shepherd whose care for his sheep was so great that he searched for the one lost little sheep until he found it, even though he had a whole flock at home (Matt. 18:10–14; Luke 15:4–7).

We already learned that Jesus is called our Shepherd, and He cares for us in the same way. But this story describes one more thing that a shepherd does: he searches for his sheep. Jesus, as our Shepherd, does the same thing. He wants us to be His so much that He loves us and searches for us until He finds us.

On Christmas, we often think of the shepherds coming to find Baby Jesus. But God took the first step! God sent His angel to find the shepherds and tell them the good news of Jesus' birth. The shepherds are a picture for us to see God's heart: God wants us to hear the good news so much that He is willing to do whatever it takes to find each person.

The Bible says, "This is how God shows His love for us; while we were still sinners, He sent Jesus Christ to die for us" (Rom. 5:8). Once again, God took the first step! The Bible says that everyone has sinned, and that when you sin, you earn death (Rom. 3:23; 6:23). But the gift God sent to us in Jesus is life (John 10:10)!

It gets even better! God took the first step toward us, then He made His gift easy to receive! Acts 16:31 says, "Believe on the Lord Jesus Christ, and you will be saved" (NKJV). All the Lord asks us to do is believe that His gift is for us and that through Jesus our sins will be wiped away! Isn't that awesome? It's so simple! All you have to do to get God's gift is to receive it!

When you do, the Bible tells us what will happen: "Now that we are set free from sin, and have become servants of God, the fruit [remember when we read about the ornaments?] of our lives will be holiness [wholeness, completeness], and we will also receive everlasting life" (Rom. 6:22).

Have you given your heart to Jesus? He is searching for you. He won't give up, either. He will search until He finds you. But now that you have heard the message, won't you, like the shepherds, come to Him and receive His gift? It's the best Christmas present you will ever receive!

December 22

Activity Page

At our house, free evenings during the month of December are few and far between! You probably have the same hectic holiday schedule at your home. But occasionally an empty evening will pop up. Maybe you planned to leave the evening free. Or maybe something was canceled. Or maybe one of the children got the sniffles and just can't go out. Whatever the reason you are home tonight, use some of the time to spend with each other.

December has the advantage of presenting some of the best family TV of the year! There are almost always fun Christmas programs on that you can enjoy as a family. If nothing appeals to you there, you could rent a Christmas video. Or pull out the kids' favorite board game. My children would spend literally hours on a good rousing game of Monopoly (with a few made-up rules allowing for bank robbery, extra turns, and building houses on each other's property!).

However, with all of the exciting things to do at Christmastime, my children's favorite "free evening" event was always making a huge bowl of popcorn, starting a fire in the fireplace, and turning out all of the lights except for the Christmas tree. They would sit, snuggle, and talk for hours—and they usually wound up bringing sleeping bags and pillows in so that they could sleep in front of the fire all night long!

Christmas Countdown

When do you need to get your turkey out to thaw? If you thaw it at room temperature, place it in the sink in cold water and allow five hours thawing time per pound. Or figure two to three days to thaw it in the refrigerator.

We have all heard the story about the wise men coming to see Baby Jesus. We picture them riding across the desert on dark, still nights. Of course, they are on camels, passing oases of palm trees, and always, always keeping the star in view straight ahead of them. After a long, hard journey, they finally arrive in Bethlehem and fall to their knees in worship of the Christ Child, presenting their gifts of gold, frankincense, and myrrh. But if we look a little more closely at the whole story, we see that the wise men are also great examples of people who stand for what they believe no matter what anyone else says, does, or thinks.

The wise men had been going about their lives as usual, when suddenly one night, a star appeared that they had never seen before. Deciding that the star was a heavenly proclamation that a king had been born, the wise men did something no one else had ever done before. They followed a star in hopes of finding this new king so that they could worship him. Were they laughed at? Did their friends think they were a little crazy? There is no way to know for certain, but we do know that no one else came with them.

After they had traveled for many months, they arrived at Jerusalem. Surely the capital city is where the new king had been born! But they found the city in an uproar over their arrival! King Herod was filled with jealousy and rage over the possibility of someone trying to usurp his throne. The priests were busy searching the Scriptures to find out where the Messiah would be born. Housewives discussed the possibility of a new king as they bargained in the marketplace. *Has the Messiah really come?* they wondered. Workmen, worried about the wrath of Rome, asked, "Will Caesar send more soldiers to crush any rumors of a new king and a possible rebellion?" And everyone gossiped about the magnificent wealth that accompanied these royal visitors from faraway lands. But in spite of the city's curiosity, none of those people came with the wise men to Bethlehem either.

Have you ever heard of peer pressure? Peer pressure is doing what everyone else is doing—even if it isn't the right thing to do or if it's something you don't want to do. No one likes to stand out in a group; no one wants to be the only one who stands against the crowd and points out what's right. We all want to be included.

But the wise men set out on a quest to find the King of kings. It involved setting aside what others thought and doing something totally different. God challenges us in the same way that He challenged the wise men. He asks each of us to follow Him completely.

After all, finding the King of kings is the best adventure ever!

December 23

Activity Page

It has been said that a nation cannot chart its future if it does not have a thorough knowledge of its past. What is true of nations is also true of families—and it is true of individuals. Psalm 78:5–7 makes it clear that we have a responsibility to tell our children not only about the commandments of the Lord but also about His works. (See also Exodus 19:3; Psalm 48:13.) We are to give them a sense of their own history and an awareness of God's personal interest in each of our lives, and there is no better way to do that than to share with them His mercies toward your family. The psalmist urges us to "declare what He has done for my soul" (Ps. 66:16, NKJV). And the writer of Hebrews exhorts us to "encourage one another daily…lest any of you be hardened through the deceitfulness of sin" (Heb. 3:13). Recounting the faithfulness of the Lord not only gives our children a sense of their own family history, but it also helps to establish them, protecting them from the influences of sin as they see God's mighty workings in their home.

One of my favorite ways to accomplish this is to take an hour or so and look through old photos. (This is an activity my children always loved.) This gives you an opportunity to share your family's history: your childhood, courtship, and marriage, and the funny things your children said and did as preschoolers. Along with those stories, tell your children the stories of how you came to know the Lord, how He has provided for you, directed you, and protected you.

Each of our children has faced life-threatening situations. We would rehearse those stories—and remind them that it is the Lord who sustained their lives! As your children get older, invite them to join in, recounting things that the Lord has done for them personally, such as how they received Jesus as their Savior and how the Lord helped them in a difficult situation. They are familiarizing themselves with what God has done for them. As they do this, they will find it more and more difficult, even impossible, to deny God's existence—because they have already seen Him at work in their lives!

We also told our children about the Lord's workings as we answered questions. One of our sons asked us about prayer and how it is answered. Not only were we able to teach him something new about life in the Lord, but we were also able to share with him ways that the Lord has answered us.

But perhaps the best way to make children aware of God's personal workings toward each of us is to let a spirit of thanksgiving permeate your home. As your children see you continually praising the Lord for the many blessings He pours out each day, they will begin to recognize His workings in each of their lives as well. What a solid foundation we are privileged to provide for our children of instruction, love, security, acceptance, and knowledge of the Lord!

Christmas Countdown

Assemble and hide all large gifts. Maybe

a neighbor could help out here. One year

we refinished a bed for our daughter and

simply declared the garage off limits for

the month of December by posting a large

sign that read, "Santa's Workshop."

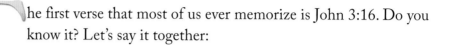

The first verse that most of us ever memorize is John 3:16. Do you know it? Let's say it together:

For God so loved the world that He gave His only begotten Son, that whoever believes in Him should not perish but have everlasting life.

When Jesus enters our lives, not only do we receive God's gift, but also we start to become like Him! That means that we become gift givers, too! We can be gift givers by telling people about Jesus. We can be gift givers by loving people and being kind. But at Christmas, we also get to be gift givers by giving presents. Isn't it fun to go shopping and pick out the perfect gift for Mom and Dad? Or maybe you made something really special at school. Wrapping up the present, then waiting for Christmas morning to arrive is so exciting! I have wondered if that isn't the same kind of excitement God feels when we receive His gifts!

The Bible tells us that God is still giving us gifts! He not only gave us Jesus, but He also gives us salvation, health, our special talents and abilities, the Bible, our family, and friends. James 1:17 says that "every good gift and every perfect gift is from above, and comes down from the Father" (NKJV). That means that every good thing that we have comes to us from God.

But when we become gift givers, it involves one more thing. In the Christmas story, we read that the wise men brought Jesus gifts. We all know about the gold, frankincense, and myrrh. Those are some awesome gifts, but most of us don't have any of those things. However, the Bible also says that the wise men worshiped Jesus.

That's something I can give Jesus! The Bible teaches us that when we give the Lord our praise and thanksgiving, we are giving an offering to Him.

Let's do that this Christmas! If we remember that God was the very first gift giver, opening presents around the Christmas tree will be a time of thankfulness—not just for the presents we receive, but for Jesus, too.

December 24

Activity Page

When it comes time to wrap gifts, take all the gift wrapping supplies and place them by the children. Not only will you enjoy the time together, but children love to wrap gifts, and they can help a lot. They can find boxes, stick on bows, and hand you pieces of tape. And you always need an extra person to hold everything secure while you tie the string! My children also enjoyed choosing which paper will go on whose gift.

Something we did with our children many times was to wrap gifts in themes. Once we wrapped everything with solid red paper and white ribbon. Sometimes we will wrap gifts by families—one kind of paper for all the gifts that go to Uncle Jack and Aunt Joann's family, another kind for Uncle Dennis and Aunt Cathy's family. One year we were so broke that we wrapped everything in plain brown paper tied with red and green yarn. Then for bows, the children stuck on bright colored leaves out of our yard!

Another thing that we enjoyed doing was decorating the outside of the boxes we mail. One year we bought different colored dot-stickers from the office supply store and stuck them all over the boxes. Then the children drew happy faces on all the dots. But usually I gave them a supply of Christmas stickers and red and green markers. (Just be sure to leave the address space clear!)

Of course, wrapping gifts with the children doesn't work when it comes to their gifts. For their presents, I try to get all of the shopping and wrapping done before school is out. If you have responsibilities during the day, try my all time favorite December "get-my-head-together-I-need-some-space-too" alone time. I will wait until everyone is asleep, turn on some of my favorite music, and wrap gifts all by myself!

And when they see their gifts all wrapped and ready, does that ever intensify the excitement!

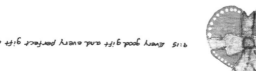

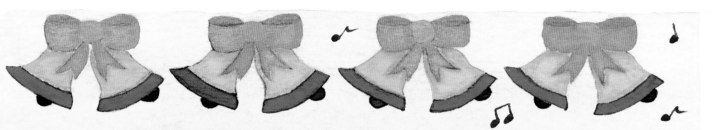

Christmas Countdown

Are you ready for the big day tomorrow?

Today is the day to make ahead any food

possible. Bake pies, prepare any dishes that can

be refrigerated, get your stuffing mixed (but

don't stuff the turkey until right before you

put it in the oven), and take out any frozen

dishes that you made earlier in the month.

December 25

These are the facts concerning the birth of Jesus Christ:

○○○○○

Before anything else existed, there was Christ, with God. And Christ became a human being and lived here on earth among us and was full of loving forgiveness and truth. And some of us have seen His glory—the glory of the only Son of the Heavenly Father.

His mother, Mary, was engaged to be married to Joseph. But while she was still a virgin she became pregnant by the Holy Spirit.

The angel Gabriel appeared to her and said:

"Don't be frightened, Mary…for God has decided to wonderfully bless you! Very soon now, you will become pregnant and have a baby boy, and you are to name Him 'Jesus.' He shall be very great and shall be called the Son of God. And the Lord God shall give him the throne of his ancestor David. And he shall reign over Israel forever; his Kingdom shall never end!"

Mary asked the angel, "But how can I have a baby? I am a virgin."

The angel replied, "The Holy Spirit shall come upon you, and the power of God shall overshadow you; so the baby born to you will be utterly holy—the Son of God.…"

Mary said, "I am the Lord's servant, and I am willing to do whatever He wants. May everything you said come true." And then the angel disappeared.…[1]

○○○○○

December 25

Then Joseph, her fiancé, being a man of stern principle, decided to break the engagement but to do it quietly, as he didn't want to publicly disgrace her. As he lay awake considering this, he fell into a dream, and saw an angel standing beside him. "Joseph, son of David," the angel said, "don't hesitate to take Mary as your wife! For the child within her has been conceived by the Holy Spirit. And she will have a Son, and you shall name him Jesus (meaning 'Savior'), for he will save his people from their sins. This will fulfill God's message through his prophets—"Listen! The virgin shall conceive a child! She shall give birth to a Son, and he shall be called 'Emmanuel' (meaning 'God is with us')."

When Joseph awoke, he did as the angel commanded.[2]

○○○○○

About this time Caesar Augustus, the Roman Emperor, decreed that a census should be taken….Everyone was required to return to his ancestral home for this registration. And because Joseph was a member of the royal line, he had to go to Bethlehem in Judea, King David's ancient home, journeying there from the Galilean village of Nazareth. He took with him Mary, his fiancée, who was obviously pregnant by this time.

And while they were there, the time came for her baby to be born; and she gave birth to her first child, a son. She wrapped him in a blanket and laid him in a manger, because there was no room for them in the village inn.

That night some shepherds were in the fields outside the village, guarding their flocks of sheep. Suddenly an angel appeared among them, and the landscape shone bright with the glory of the Lord....

"Don't be afraid!" he [the angel] said. "I bring you the most joyful news ever announced, and it is for everyone! The Savior—yes, the Messiah, the Lord—has been born tonight in Bethlehem! How will you recognize him? You will find a baby wrapped in a blanket, lying in a manger!" Suddenly, the angel was joined by a vast host of others—the armies of heaven—praising God: "Glory to God in the highest heaven," they sang, "and peace on earth for all those pleasing to him."

When this great army of angels had returned again to heaven, the shepherds said to each other, "Come on! Let's go to Bethlehem! Let's see this wonderful thing that has happened, which the Lord has told us about."

They ran to the village and found their way to Mary and Joseph. And there was the baby, lying in the manger....Then the shepherds went back again to their fields and flocks, praising God for the visit of the angels, and because they had seen the child, just as the angel had told them.[3]

○○○○○

At about that time some [wise men] from eastern lands arrived in Jerusalem, asking, "Where is the newborn King of the Jews? For we have seen his star in far-off eastern lands, and have come to worship him."

King Herod was deeply disturbed by their question, and all Jerusalem was filled with rumors. He called a meeting of the Jewish religious leaders. "Did the prophets tell us where the Messiah would be born?" he asked.

"Yes, in Bethlehem," they said, "for this is what the Prophet Micah wrote: 'O little town of Bethlehem, you are not just an unimportant Judean village, for a Governor shall rise from you to rule my people Israel."

Then Herod sent a private message to the [wise men]....He told them, "Go to Bethlehem and search for the child. And when you find him, come back and tell me so that I can go and worship him too!" After this interview the [wise men] started out again. And look! The star appeared to them again, standing over Bethlehem. Their joy knew no bounds!

Entering the house where the baby and Mary his mother were, they threw themselves down before him, worshiping. Then they opened their presents and gave him gold, frankincense and myrrh.[4]

○○○○○

Eight days later, at the baby's circumcision ceremony, he was named Jesus, the name given him by the angel before he was even conceived....

God...gave him a name which is above every other name, that at the name of Jesus every knee shall bow in heaven and on earth and under the earth, and every tongue shall confess that Jesus Christ is Lord, to the glory of God the Father.[5]

[1]LUKE 1:30–38, THE LIVING BIBLE
[2]MATTHEW 1:19–24, THE LIVING BIBLE
[3]LUKE 2:1–20, THE LIVING BIBLE
[4]MATTHEW 2:1–11, THE LIVING BIBLE
[5]LUKE 2:21; PHILIPPIANS 2:9–11, THE LIVING BIBLE

Christmas morning is usually so full of activity that I try to keep breakfast simple, yet Christmas is also a special day, and so I want to have something special. But "special" is basically anything we don't usually have. Our Christmas morning breakfasts have ranged from the super simple—like doughnuts and hot chocolate, to the more involved with quiche, muffins, and fruit salad, to our oldest son making blueberry waffles one Christmas morning for everyone with one of his Christmas gifts: a Snoopy waffle iron! Here are some ideas to keep your morning meal simple AND special.

For Christmas morning breakfast, make sure that you've done all of your menu planning and grocery shopping by December 22. This allows you to make as much as possible ahead of time on December 23. The year we served quiche, we had two dozen relatives at our house—that's a lot of quiche! But we made the quiches about a week ahead and froze them. Then on Christmas morning, they just went into the oven while we opened gifts. Simple—yet special!

Other easy or make-ahead breakfasts are waffles (either homemade or the pop-in-the-toaster type), pie (I claim that these are no different than fruit-filled pastries), or cereal (let the kids pick something just for fun).

Some families don't like standard breakfast fare. If this is the case with your family, try something like a pizza, but shape the crust like a Christmas tree. Vegetable-filled omelets or turkey and cranberry sauce sandwiches might also be workable suggestions for you.

Just remember that in the midst of making things "special," don't lose the "simple." Enjoy your breakfast…and let the holiday begin!

Christmas Countdown

You have seen pictures in magazines; you have seen it on TV; you have read hints in the paper on how to roast those tender, succulent, juicy turkeys that melt in your mouth! So why is accomplishing this in the privacy of our own homes so complicated for most of us?

The major reason we turn out dry turkey after dry turkey is that we remember Grandma roasting her turkeys for hours and hours—all night in fact! The difference is that with modern poultry-raising techniques, turkeys don't need to roast forever to become tender. In fact, they need to roast less to stay juicy! The following chart will give you a good idea of how long to roast your turkey.

Time Table for Roasting	
Oven temp. 325°	
WEIGHT	**MINUTES PER POUND**
Under 8 pounds	25–30
8–16 pounds	20–25
Over 16 pounds	No more than 7 hours total

What About "After" the 25 Days 'Til Christmas?

The week between Christmas and New Year's Day tends to be a "lost" week for many people. Very few things are scheduled for this week, and our tendency is to lie around and gaze in dismay at our dried-up Christmas trees and punch-stained carpets!

One year, however, I decided to redeem this last week of December so that our family could begin the new year with a "clean slate."

Here's some suggestions for you to consider:

1. Undecorate the house. When I do this, I repair or clean up anything that needs it so I don't have to mess with it during a busy next December.

2. Evaluate how everything went this year. Write down whatever comes to mind that would make the holidays go more smoothly next year. This could be as simple as remembering to buy more ice, or as involved as planning an open house.

3. Find places to put away all of the gifts. This is a project in itself—especially with kids' stuff! Get this out of the way during this week, and at the same time try to get the children's closets straightened up (again!).

4. Write your thank-you notes. After the New Year when everything is back in full swing, you won't feel like it!

5. Enjoy your family. This week generally doesn't require much of anybody, so spend time together. You may want to consider arranging a few vacation days during this time—and that makes it even better!

6. Spend time with the Lord. At the end of each year, spend some time talking to Jesus about the past year and what He wants your personal and family vision and goals to be for the coming year. Write these down in a letter to Him, and review it a year later. It's amazing to watch how He answers and brings things to fulfillment—from losing that five pounds gained during December to the salvation of a dear friend. Present all of those things to Him!

And as you do, it is my prayer that this book will continue to be a blessing to your family for many Christmases to come…and happy new year!

Expanded Christmas Card List

Use these two pages to list the people whom you send Christmas cards to each year. Suggestion: Write in pencil, because names and addresses have a way of changing frequently.

Name	Address	City	State	Zip

Name	Address	City	State	Zip

Expanded Christmas Shopping List

Use these two pages to complete your gift shoppping lists. Don't forget to include party supplies and other holdiay items that you will need to purchase.

GIFT OR SUPPLIES	DETAILS (recipient, color, size, where to purchase, etc.)	DONE!

GIFT OR SUPPLIES	DETAILS (recipient, color, size, where to purchase, etc.)	DONE!

Expanded Holiday Baking Preparations

List all the recipes that you will be using for your holiday menus. Include the cookies you make, the menu recipes for your holiday meals, and special recipes like spiced apple cider and your favorite homemade candies.

Recipe	Occasion

List all the ingredients you need to purchase for your holiday preparations. Check your pantry and spice shelves first, making sure the supplies you have are really still there—and really fresh!

Ingredients	For